The Role of the Teacher

by Eric Hoyle

Department of Education,
University of Manchester

LONDON AND HENLEY
ROUTLEDGE & KEGAN PAUL
NEW YORK: HUMANITIES PRESS

9532

First published 1969
by Routledge & Kegan Paul Ltd
39 Store Street
London WC1E 7DD,
296 Beaconsfield Parade, Middle Park
Melbourne 3206, Australia and
Broadway House, Newtown Road
Henley-on-Thames, Oxon RG9 1EN
Reprinted 1969 (twice), 1970, 1972, 1975, 1980 and 1982
Printed and bound in Great Britain
by T.J. Press (Padstow) Ltd,
Padstow, Cornwall
© Eric Hoyle 1969
ISBN 0 7100 6435 7 (C)
ISBN 0 7100 6436 5 (P)

The Role of the Teacher

THE STUDENTS LIBRARY OF EDUCATION has been designed to meet the needs of students of Education at Colleges of Education and at University Institutes and Departments. It will also be valuable for practising teachers and educationists. The series takes full account of the latest developments in teacher-training and of new methods and approaches in education. Separate volumes will provide authoritative and up-to-date accounts of the topics within the major fields of sociology, philosophy and history of education, educational psychology, and method. Care has been taken that specialist topics are treated lucidly and usefully for the non-specialist reader. Altogether, the Students Library of Education will provide a comprehensive introduction and guide to anyone concerned with the study of education and with educational theory and practice.

J. W. TIBBLE

There are now some 350,000 teachers working in maintained primary and secondary schools; soon there will be half a million. If we include all those who teach in further and higher education, in schools outside the state system, in the services and in industry, the overall number is larger still. Teachers are, in fact, one of the largest occupational groups in our society, but their numbers and importance has not been reflected in the amount of attention that has been given to them by social scientists and research workers.

In this book Eric Hoyle shows how the modes of description and analysis employed by the sociologist of education can throw light upon the teacher's role in classroom, in school and in society. Existing studies of the teacher's role are mainly in the form of research reports and scattered articles. The evidence and conceptual threads drawn together in this book contribute towards a systematic analysis of the role of the teacher that will be of value to both the intending teacher and the experienced educationist.

WILLIAM TAYLOR

Contents

1

The teacher's role in cultural perspective

The central concern of this book is with the role of the teacher in contemporary Britain. This will be examined in the context of the classroom, the school, the local community, and the wider society. But before proceeding it will be advantageous to contrast the role of the teacher in a technological society such as Britain with the role which he has performed in pre-industrial society. Teachers in all societies and at all times have faced common problems, but the industrialization of a society commits its educational system to a new set of functions and its teachers to a changing role.

Learning in primitive societies

The child begins to learn the ways of his society from birth. He learns the patterns of behaviour which are expected of him, and these expectations embody the values of his society which he tends to *internalize* and make his own. These values are an important part of the culture of the group, and he will also learn other elements of this culture: language, customs, beliefs, the use of tools and utensils, the working of institutions, literature, folklore, music and many other things. He will learn part of this culture informally through observing, imitating, participating and so forth, earning approval for successful learning and disapproval when he deviates from expectations. He learns from his parents, his brothers and sisters, and other members of the group, and he may also be taught more directly how to make or do something by an adult member of the group. But primitive societies do not as a rule have 'teachers' in the sense of persons whose specialized role in society is to instruct the young. The child acquires a knowledge of his culture through the process of *socialization*, and in these societies socialization is synonymous with education; it involves learning but little teaching. A distinction can be drawn between the socialization of the pre-adolescent and the adolescent in a primitive society. Before the age of puberty, the child learns in the informal way described above, but with the onset of adolescence socialization becomes much more formalized through what have been called the *rites de passage*, ceremonies which mark the child's initiation into adult society. During this period, he is given more formal instruction in the historical and religious aspects of the culture of his tribe. He is taught the tribe's view of its own origin and history, the nature and qualities of the tribal gods, the tribal myths, legends and stories. He is instructed in the ceremonials of the tribe and learns to play appropriate roles in these. The emphasis is on the sacredness of the tribal culture and the purpose is to make the adolescent a conforming adult member of his tribe. Instruction in the ceremonials stresses the need to perform these in precisely the 'right' way, any deviation in phrasing, movement or sequence being held to spoil the ritual. Tradition and the changeless pattern of life is stressed. There is nothing lighthearted or carefree about this part of the child's socialization. It is, however, significant that with some exceptions there is little instruction in the practical arts nor in how to gain a living. The transmission of values and instruction in the rituals which embody them are at the core of the process of socialization, other elements in the child's education are left very much to chance. The anthropologist, C. W. M. Hart (1955) has made the following comment on this situation:

> Hunting, gardening, cattle-tending, fishing, are not taught at the boy's initiation; he has already learnt the rudiments of these at home in his intimate groups before initiation starts. This is a surprising finding because of the well-known fact that many of these people live pretty close to starvation point and none of them manage to extract much more than a subsistence from their environment. But despite this, the cultures in question are blissfully ignorant of economic determinism, and blandly leave instruction in basic food production to the laissez faire, casual hit or miss teaching of parents, friends, play-groups, etc. When society forcibly takes over a boy in order to make him into a man and teach him the things a man should know, it is not concerned with teaching him to be a better gardener or tender of cattle or fisherman, even though the economic survival of the tribe clearly depends upon one or other of these occupations. The initiation curricula cover instead quite different series of subjects which I am tempted to call 'cultural subjects' in either sense of the word 'culture'.

This emphasis on the transmission of values through the normal processes of socialization and relative neglect of the economic functions of education in primitive societies is, as we shall see, in great contrast to the functions of education in an industrialized society. The distinctive role of the teacher has not emerged, and the instruction given in connection with a boy's initiation is undertaken by appropriate members of the tribe, perhaps, for example, the boy's senior male cross-cousins. In order to emphasize the sacredness of the initiation and distinguish it from the easy-going pre-pubertal socialization, the 'appropriate' people are often members of the tribe who are strangers, or relative strangers, to the boy.

This sketch of socialization in primitive society has been necessarily brief and oversimplified. There are, in fact some exceptions to the point made that 'teachers' are not to be found in this sort of society. One of the most interesting of these exceptions occurs in some parts of West Africa where 'bush' schools, or *poro* schools, are established. The educative units of West Africa have been the 'secret societies' into which both boys and girls are initiated. For the purpose of initiation 'schools' are established in the forest away from the tribe and here the novice lives for a 'term' which varies in length from area to area but lasts on the average for two years. Here he is instructed in the history and mythology of the tribe, the nature of its social relationships, its lore, its arts and crafts. The teaching is accompanied by opportunities for practice in house-building, tracking animals, fighting mock battles, and carrying out many of the normal activities of tribal life. Some children are given special instruction in crafts for which they show a special aptitude. The school is presided over by a 'teacher' of whom Watkins (1963) writes:

> He has majestic status in the society, is respected by the chief and elders of the tribe, and is honoured with intense devotion by the youth of the land. In personal characteristics he must be chivalrous, courteous, public-spirited, law-abiding, and fearless. He must have full knowledge of all the native lore, arts and crafts, and must be well-versed in the history and traditions of his people and an authentic judge of all matters affecting their welfare. Other men of good repute who are specialists in various fields of activity serve as assistants and teachers of the novices.

The status of the grandmaster of the bush school is clearly very high, and attaches to him as the embodiment of the values of his tribe rather than to his skill as a teacher. It is dependent as much on what he *is* as on what he *knows*. He is valued not as a specialist but as the type of man idealized by the tribe. Although he supervises the transmission of skills, in any case a rather unusual function in a primitive society, his main function is to produce 'good members of his tribe. In transmitting the traditional values of the tribe, he is performing an essentially conservative function.

A much more distinctive teaching role emerges in what have been called 'intermediate' societies. These are societies which, although not industrialized, are more complex than primitive societies in that there is a more widespread division of labour and a hierarchy of social groupings enjoying differing degrees of prestige. These societies include archaic societies such as ancient Egypt, 'historic' intermediate empires such as China, India and the Roman Empire, and the 'seed-bed' societies of Israel and Greece (Parsons, 1966). An important characteristic of these societies is that the groups with the highest social status—the elite—were literate and developed their own 'high' culture which was not accessible to the mass of the population. In such societies one of the social functions of education becomes the transmission of the culture of elite groups to their children. Those who transmit this knowledge are undoubtedly 'teachers', but this role was often subsidiary to the role of priest, philosopher, or learned and literate man. In India there was a long tradition whereby the guru, or wise man, had a number of pupils constantly in attendance at his side. In Athens the philosopher-teacher had his heyday, and in medieval Europe he was frequently a priest. These priests and men of knowledge not only taught the neophytes who were to follow them into their calling, but also the children of the elite groups. There were undoubtedly many reasons why the leading groups in all societies wished their children to be educated by the learned men, but two of these can be singled out as having a special relevance in this context. Firstly, education was a source of distinction between the higher and lower groups. This was most pronounced where it was transmitted in a language such as Latin and Sanskrit which was not known by the mass of the population. Secondly, the elite groups wished their children to learn the traditional knowledge of their society, particularly those traditional values which were a justification of the *status quo*. Thus the transmission of knowledge and the training of the intellect was inextricably mixed with the inculcation of the predominant values of the society, and the fate of the philosopher-teacher Socrates is an indication of the view taken of men whose teaching undermined the established order. In some societies the teacher visited the boy's home to instruct him, but where schools were established as distinctive institutions the father would take care to ensure that the teacher was inculcating the 'appropriate' values. In Athens the boy was accompanied to school by his *paedogogos*, or tutor, who was one of his father's servants, and he sat with the boy in school whilst he did his lessons. In Ronal Dore's highly relevant and fascinating book *Education in Tokugawa Japan* there is an illustration of a visit made to a fief school by the *shogun* who governed the fief and sent his sons to the school. The picture makes quite clear the father's concern with what was being transmitted.

The importance of the transmission of values as compared with the teaching of skills is clearly seen when we examine a form of education which might superficially be regarded as truly vocational—the education of the mandarin in Classical China. This was essentially an education for administrative position in the civil service. The aim an elite parent was to gain for his child a position in the hierarchy of officialdom and this was achieved by displaying a knowledge of the traditional forms of etiquette governing the conduct of affairs. The system was highly competitive with three levels of degree roughly corresponding with our own B.A., M.A., and Ph.D. Candidates were taught in schools by teachers who had themselves either failed to gain a position in the mandarinate and had turned to teaching as an alternative form of occupation, or had turned to it temporarily whilst waiting hopefully for such a post. The future mandarin did not, however, acquire the technical knowledge necessary for the administration of a locality. What he did acquire was a knowledge of etiquette which marked him as being a gentleman. What he learnt from his teacher was a knowledge of the *li*, the traditional forms of etiquette which symbolized social relationships and embodied the social duties with which the child had already been becoming acquainted within his family. The mandarin thus embodied a set of traditional values, and we see that the function of the teacher whose task it was to inculcate these was essentially conservative. Just as the adolescent in a primititive society needed to become word-perfect in the rituals of his tribe, the neophyte mandarin had to become infallible in his knowledge of etiquette. Such practical knowledge as accounting could safely be left to the clerks who would acquire it on the job.

N.B.   The main point which is being made in this chapter— that the role of the teacher in pre-industrial societies was concerned with the transmission of a 'high' culture and a particular set of values to the children of elite groups— is reinforced if we examine the history of the role of the British teacher before the onset of industrialization. His major function was to transmit a body of unchanging knowledge, primarily a knowledge of classical languages and literatures, to the future elite. Frequently the teacher was also a clergyman and taught in the public and grammar schools. His clientele was the sons of the aristocracy, or rather those who were not privately tutored at home, and the sons of the squirearchy and members of the professional classes who sought careers in the church, politics, administration or another of the professions. For these a knowledge of Latin was essential. It was an education which was 'vocational' in the sense of giving the pupils the 'cultural style' which was a prerequisite to entry into one of the professions, but it in no way provided any occupational expertise. It was also concerned with the transmission of the values embodied in the Christian religion—or at least a certain interpretation of these —and the more generalized values held by the ruling groups. This tradition persists in the grammar schools and public schools today and is to some extent in conflict with the demands made upon education arising out the rapid technological developments of recent years. The education which the future administrators of the British Empire received in the public schools has been compared with the education of the Chinese mandarin referred to above (Wilkinson, 1966). Both were concerned with the inculcation of a basic set of values rather than with instruction in the arts of administration. Britain's technological progress was perhaps more an outcome of the alternative curricula which were developed in the private and 'Dissenting' academies which grew up in the eighteenth century to provide an education for those children who were barred from Anglican schools on religious grounds. Nicholas Hans (1951) has attributed the swing to the teaching of science and the practical arts in these schools to three independent motives: religious, intellectual and utilitarian. Natural science was taught on the principle of *propagatio fidei per scientas*, the propagation of faith through science. The great upsurge of scientific knowledge during this period, much of it due to the efforts of private gentleman-scholars, encouraged the schools to broaden the classical curriculum, and the spate of invention encouraged the inclusion of such vocational subjects as navigation, accountancy and surveying. The proprietors and teachers of the academies still tended to be clergymen, but many were secular scholars who had graduated from Oxford or Cambridge. Hans quotes the following:

> John Hyde had an Academy at the end of the eighteenth century and the beginning of the nineteenth at Stroud, Gloucestershire. 'Taught English Grammar, writing for law and trade, arithmetic and merchant accounts. Geometry, trigonometry, mechanics, optics, algebra and fluxions with other useful branches of mathematics, rhetoric, geography and the use of globes.'

Thus during this period the function of cultural transmission was broadened to include a scientific element and a greater concern with the teaching of technical and vocational skills. But this broadened curriculum was still largely confined to the children of the middle classes and the teacher's role did not undergo any profound change. Although during the nineteenth century formal education became more accessible to middle class groups, it was only with the Education Act of 1870 that the foundations of a system of mass elementary education were laid with a resulting modification of the teacher's role. A variety of social forces led to the passing of this Act: a belief in the need to educate the voters in an emergent democracy, a belief in the need to 'gentle the masses' and take the edge off any revolutionary tendencies, a belief in the need for more people to be able to read the Bible, a growing awareness that the socialization of the child could no longer be fully achieved in the home, and a belief in universal education as a matter of social justice. But highly significant was the recognition of the need for a literate and numerate population in a society undergoing a period of rapid industrialization. When introducing the Bill, W. E. Forster said: 'Upon the speedy process of elementary education in England depends our industrial prosperity.' Education thus takes on new and crucial functions, and in order to understand just how these affected the teacher's role it is necessary to examine briefly some of the social changes which accompanied the process of industrialization.

The effects of industrialization

We can look first at the phenomenon of the increasing demand for skilled manpower. The first industrial revolution generated a demand for skilled artisans as well as semi-skilled and unskilled workers and for these it was believed that an elementary education, and education designed principally to spread literacy and numeracy, was

9

adequate. But as industry entered the technological phase the growing demand for skilled capacity at all levels of the occupational structure involved education in a much closer relationship with the economy. Apart from raising the general level of skills, education has been faced with the task of preparing people for a wider range of skills with the development of new industries such as electronics, and the use of new techniques in some of the older industries. There has also occurred an upgrading of labour as the demand for skilled capacity has elevated in status and responsibility people whose educational attainments would not have led them to occupy their present positions even a few years previously. The profound effect which these changes have had upon the functions of the school and the role of the teacher has been to elevate the importance of the processes of 'selection' and 'differentiation' whereby children are guided along different educational pathways in accordance with their potential occupational status. It is true that the school has always been an avenue of social and occupational mobility which has allowed the bright working-class boy to achieve a status higher than that of his father, but this process has now become a normal pattern and there has developed a whole apparatus of tests, exams and other selective devices for channelling children, even in the comprehensive school, towards different occupational categories. This is in complete contrast with pre-industrial societies in which social differentiation was dependent upon one's social background rather than on the proof of technical competence. These trends in our society have been described by great ironical skill by Michael Young in his book *The Rise of the Meritocracy*.

A second important feature of an industrialized society which has an effect upon education is the pressure towards 'bureaucratization'. Accompanying the process of industrialization has been the tendency for many of the functions formerly performed by the family or community agencies to be taken over by the state. At the same time there has been the tendency for organizations such as factories, hospitals and schools to increase in size. The term bureaucracy is often used in a pejorative sense as when it is equated with 'red tape', but as Max Weber, the great student of bureaucracy, has shown, it is an essential feature of all large scale organizations and an inevitable and necessary trend in all industrialized societies. Increasing size and specialization has led to the bureaucratization of schools which has changed the nature of schools and created new problems of cultural transmission.

Thirdly, the revolution in transport and communications, the increasing complexity of the division of labour, and increased occupational and social mobility have had social effects which have profoundly affected the process of education. The fact that the entire adult population has become the electorate has raised questions concerning the role of the school in political socialization. The functions of the family and the local community as socializing agencies have changed and some have been taken over by the school. And the media of mass communication have become significant forces with which the school has to contend. The many implications of these changes will be discussed in different parts of the book, and at this point we need only note that they have greatly affected the educational enterprise.

Conclusion

The broad changes which have occurred in the role of the teacher with the transition from pre-industrial to industrial society can be summarized as follows.

The teacher in the pre-industrial society was pre-eminently concerned with the transmission of values. By and large, the transmission of skills occurred informally. The teacher in the industrialized society, on the other hand, is necessarily orientated towards preparing children for their future occupational roles which, in spite of the advantages of birth which still persist, are very much more open to talent.

The teacher in the pre-industrial society was essentially a *conservative* agent in that he largely transmitted traditional knowledge. The teacher in the industrialized society is still, to some degree, a conservative agent, especially when concerned with younger children, but as technological societies are geared to continuous innovation, there are pressures towards a more open-ended form of education permitting the flexibility in skills which a society such as ours now requires. This is paralleled in values. Parents look to the teacher as a custodian of traditional values and to a large extent these expectations are met, but even in the sphere of values the rapidity of social change induces pressures towards flexibility. Different social groups hold different sets of values and the 'central core', if such exists, is far from being self-evident to the teacher. In pre-industrial societies, the values which were transmitted were the value of elite groups and much more easily discerned by the teacher.

There has been a shift from the pre-industrial teacher's concern with elite groups to a concern with the mass of the population. In our society, with the exception of public and selective grammar schools, the teacher has to take all comers, and as he can no longer rely upon support of the home for his values, his authority has to be earned by virtue of his personal skills whereas the authority of his predecessor was largely institutionalized.

There has been a shift from an emphasis on learning to an emphasis on teaching (although it must be admitted that the teacher is now much more concerned to set up learning situations than to teach by direct methods). The teacher in the pre-industrial society was often a wise man a learned man, a religious man, a good man or a combination of these. He was esteemed because he embodied certain values and pupils were sent to him to catch something of his qualities. With the extension of education during the industrial period and the growth of a profession of specialized teachers, there is a greater emphasis on the actual skills of teaching.

The explosion of knowledge during the industrial period has made it necessary for the contemporary teacher to be much more selective than his predecessors in what he teaches. Moreover, this growth in knowledge has been accompanied by its 'democratization'. The former aristocratic view of knowledge as somehow 'sacred' has given way to the need to disseminate knowledge much more widely and a growth in the belief that we have by no means reached, and probably never will, the limit of what the mass of the population can gain from education. This has affected the teacher's role in that there are pressures upon him to accept no level as final in the dissemination of knowledge.

Although considerable restrictions remain, there has been a movement away from what might be called an 'agreed syllabus' to a system whereby the teacher has greater autonomy in deciding what should be given priority in the curriculum. Comparing this situation with that which existed in primitive society, Margaret Mead has written (1963):

> There are several striking differences between our concept of education today and that of any contemporary primitive society; but perhaps the most important one is the shift from the need for an individual to learn something which everyone agrees he would wish to know, to the will of some individual to teach something which it is not agreed that anyone has any desire to know.

The significance of these changes for the contemporary teacher will be discussed in the following chapter.

2

The teacher's role in an industrial society

We can summarize as follows the major social functions and corresponding roles of the teacher in an industrialized society.

Instruction. The teacher transmits a body of knowledge and skills appropriate to the abilities and needs of the child. He performs this function through direct teaching and by organizing learning situations of a less formal kind. The appropriate role is that of 'teacher-as-instructor' which is the most obvious and public of the teacher's roles.

Socialization. The teacher prepares the child for participating in the way of life of his society. This process involves some instruction since, for example, the acquisition of literacy and numeracy can be regarded as an essential part of the socialization process. The values and norms of society can also be taught directly to some extent. But instruction and socialization cannot be fully equated as the inculcation of values and norms—the basis of the socialization process—cannot occur wholly, or even largely, through direct and explicit teaching. It is often said that values are 'caught and not taught' which rightly suggests that they are acquired in subtle ways in the process of teacher-pupil interaction. Success in encouraging children to internalize a particular set of values depends to a great extent upon the teacher's own embodiment of these values. The appropriate role is thus 'teacher-as-model'.

Evaluation. The teacher differentiates children on the basis of their intellectual—and often social—skills in preparation for the social and occupational roles which they will eventually play. The appropriate role is 'teacher-as-judge'. He enacts this role in ways which include recommending promotions and demotions within the school, nominating children to take certain external examinations, and counselling children and their parents with regard to appropriate school courses, further education courses, and employment possibilities. The judgments made by the teacher are of the greatest importance not least because they tend to become 'self-fulfilling prophesies' in that within limits children tend to meet the expectations which the teacher holds of them. Thus 'bright' children become brighter and 'dull' children duller; 'good' children become better and 'bad' children become worse. (Good examples are given in Hargreaves, 1967).

At the infant stage of education socialization is the most significant function of the teacher. The infant teacher is concerned with inculcating acceptable standards of social behaviour, teaching the fundamental skills of literacy and numeracy, transmitting a core of general knowledge, and encouraging pupils to acquire the *skills* of learning and to accept the *value* of learning. This process continues at the primary stage of education, but at this stage instruction and evaluation begin to become more significant. At the secondary stage there is a much more obvious swing towards instruction and evaluation, although socialization remains a significant task for the teacher of the adolescent.

Although teachers have other social functions such as the promotion of welfare and the fostering of autonomy (Blyth, 1965), our chief concern in this chapter will be to examine the problems facing the teacher as he tries to fulfil the three major functions and reconcile their corresponding roles. We will examine in turn: the changing value context within which teachers are working, the problems faced in teaching children from very different social backgrounds in the same school and in the same class, some of the problems which face the teacher as 'model', and we will look finally at some of the pressures which are modifying the teacher's orientation towards his task.

The value context of the teacher's role

At any point in time every society is permeated by a particular set of values which shape, and are shaped by, the major institutions—the economy, politics, religion, education, etc. These values are not static and clearly periods of value change create dilemmas for the teacher. In considering the shifts in value which are affecting the teacher in Britain at the present time, a comparison with the American situation will be helpful. It has been suggested that American society is permeated by the values of *equality* and *achievement*, whereas British society is dominated by the values of *elitism* (i.e. a belief in the general superiority of a few individuals over the many) and *ascription* (i.e. an emphasis placed on status due to birth, wealth or some other ascribed criterion rather than on individual achievement). Thus the values permeating British society are the opposite of those which permeate American society (Lipset, 1963). It is further held that these values have shaped the educational systems of both countries. Equalitarianism has not in the past greatly affected the British educational system. Whereas in America the school system sprang from the grassroots of local communities, in Britain a national system of education was handed down from above. Different types of secondary school have, for the most part, educated children from corresponding social strata, and have reinforced the class structure rather than modified it.

Primary schools have educated children from a wider variety of social backgrounds but since one of the functions of the primary school has been to allocate children to different types of secondary education, equality has been very narrowly conceived. One role of the teacher in the public sector of education has been to motivate the bright child to acquire a place in the grammar school which, if he was from a working class background, would set him on the road to a higher social status. Within the grammar school part of the role of the teacher is to motivate children to gain entry to the university and thus enhance their chances of gaining elite status. The development of *formal* equality of opportunity did not overcome the problem of children having an unequal start through coming from homes in which education was not valued and there was little motivation to achieve success at school. Although teachers in the secondary modern schools, the schools attended by the larger part of the population, did much to raise the education levels of their pupils, the system itself was working against them in many ways (Taylor, 1963). It can be argued that the 'ladder' represented equality of opportunity in that there were no barriers to the bright child who was motivated towards high academic achievement, but for some children the ladder was, in fact, an escalator, whilst for others it was more like a greasy pole. The role of the teacher has been influenced by the elitist values pervading the educational system, and on the whole he has perhaps been committed to promoting the able rather than securing advance along a broad front. The American value system embodies a very different concept of equality. Equality (at least between white citizens) has been a much-proclaimed value amongst Americans many of whom emigrated to America in order to escape various forms of inequality in their countries of origin. The strength of this value, added to the fact that American schools tended to originate as a community enterprise, has resulted in the

American system of education being less concerned with selecting the elite than with promoting an overall educational advancement. In his study of the American value system, Lipset (1963) has written:

> This equalitarian liberalism was perhaps strongest in the school system, where educators carried the idea of equal treatment to a point where even intellectual differences were ignored. Special encouragement of the gifted child was regarded as an unfair privilege that inflicted psychic punishment on the less gifted: personality adjustment for *all* became the objective. In New York City, Fiorello La Guardia, the militant progressive mayor, abolished Townsend Harris High School—a special school for gifted boys in which four years work was completed in three—on the grounds that the very existence of such a school was undemocratic, because it conferred special privileges on a minority.

Turner (1961) has shown how differences in the basic value systems of Britain and America are reflected in their educational systems, and has called the British system one of 'sponsored mobility' in which 'elite recruits are chosen by established elites or their agents, and elite status is *given* on the basis of some criterion of supposed merit and cannot be *taken* by any amount of effort or strategy' and the American system as one of 'contest mobility' 'in which elite status is a prize in an open contest and is taken by the aspirants' own efforts.' Thus in the British system the teacher acts as an agent of the elite (although no one suggests that this is how he consciously conceives his role) whilst in the American system the role of the teacher is to hold the ring in a fair contest.

The 'ascription-achievement' distinction between British and American values is closely associated with the 'elitist-equalitarian' distinction. In fact, societies with ascriptive values are necessarily also elitist. The ascriptive aspects of British education can easily be seen in such examples as the greater chances of a boy from a public school

18

than a boy from a grammar school with the same A level achievements getting a place at Oxford or Cambridge because he is more inclined to apply to these universities. Similiarly, there is a widespread view that an Oxbridge degree is 'better' than a degree from a Redbrick, that the latter is better than a C.A.T. degree, that a grammar school G.C.E. is 'better' than a secondary modern G.C.E. —given the same level of performance in each case. In short, the sort of educational institution attended— and this is, in any case, highly related to the social class background of parents—is often of more significance than what is achieved there.

In an industrialized society with a highly complex division of labour, it is essential that occupational roles are allocated on the basis of capacity. Thus achievement is a more appropriate value than ascription from the point of view of efficiency. As educational qualifications are increasingly becoming the basis for the allocation of occupational roles, it follows that the educational system should be pervaded by this value. It also follows that there must be no artificial handicaps to the development of capacity which implies the importance of the value of educational opportunity. There are indications that the British system of education is becoming more influenced by the values of achievement and equality of opportunity which is reflected in the moves towards comprehensive education, 'de-streaming', etc. (although it would not be correct to say that there had been any *radical* shift in values). Talcott Parsons (1961) has suggested that in a society with these values, there is no necessary conflict between the functions of instruction, selection and socialization. He writes:

> The essential point, then, seems to be that the elementary school, regarded in the light of its socializing function, is an agency which differentiates the school class broadly along the single continuum of achievement, the content of which is relative excellence in coming up to the

expectations imposed by the teacher as an agent of adult society. The criteria of this achievement are, generally speaking, undifferentiated into the cognitive or technical component and the moral or 'social' component. But with respect to its bearing on societal values, it is broadly a differentation of *levels* of capacity to act in accordance with these values.

In other words, the child at the primary stage is not judged according to his educational achievement separately from his social behaviour, he is judged according to a single criterion of achievement which involves both. As Halsey (1963) has succinctly put it, 'both goodness and cleverness are rewarded'. According to Parsons, it is at the secondary level of education when the academic achievement emerges as a separate criterion and becomes used as the basis of selection. But as Halsey points out, this analysis takes little account of the problem of children coming from different home backgrounds having very different cognitive capacities and social values. The application of the same single measuring rod to all children could well favour those who had internalized the 'appropriate' values. The re-organization of the system of education can only provide the framework within which higher achievements of all levels of intellectual capacity can be fostered. But the institutional move from 'ascriptive elitism' to 'achievement equalitarianism' does not necessarily guarantee a reorientation of the attitudes of all teachers.

The fundamental American problem is different from the British problem. The pressures on American teachers are for him to ensure that all children get equality of treatment, and insofar as his own values are centred on academic achievement and the promotion of an intellectual elite, he will experience some role conflict. This conflict is to some extent inevitable since another crucial value in American society is individual achievement. The mythus of 'log cabin to White House' has dominated

American attitudes, and as education becomes the central avenue of social mobility replacing the self-made business career or political career, it becomes a significant value for education. The pursuit of equality *and* individual achievement creates a conflict for the teacher because individual achievement leads to inequality. As T. H. Marshall (1950) has pointed out, equality of opportunity implies the opportunity to become unequal. This has been less of a problem for the British teacher since inequality has been built into the system itself. In the past the American teacher has tended to foster the social adjustment of all children rather than promoting individual academic excellence. The school report which the child took home frequently reported upon his sociability and helpfulness, but did not indicate his academic grades. Richard Hofstadter (1964) has brilliantly analysed the anti-intellectualism in American education during the 'progressive' period when the major role of the teacher was conceived as being to secure the 'life-adjustment' of his pupils in purely social terms. But with the launching of the first Russian sputnik there was an intensification of the criticism of American education for its misplaced equalitarianism. It became recognized that in order to be a competitive technological society, America could no longer allow highly skilled scientists and technologists to study frivolous subjects in high school and university, nor rely upon them 'emerging' from the highly democratic process of education. There has been a growing view that talent must be detected and cultivated wherever it is found. Hence the role of the American teacher is undergoing some change as it becomes expected of him that he will not only foster equality but will also sponsor academic excellence. The conflict within the American system of education, and the role conflict which besets the teacher is indicated by the question: 'Can we be equal and excellent too?' which is the sub-title of a book by J. W. Gardner (1961) which discusses these changes. It has been argued by David Riesman (1957) that the teacher's role must now be 'counter-cyclical' since within the cycles of value change which occur in education, it is the function of the teacher to work against the trend. He believes that at the present time this means that the American teacher must wage a battle against mediocrity and emphasize the importance of intellectual achievement, thus relinquishing his 'progressive' role which was, in its day, a valuable antidote to a sterile form of education.

Thus, although the teacher's role in Britain and America has been governed by different values, there are indications that certain common problems—economic in origin—are leading to a convergence. The British system is becoming more equalitarian and flexible whilst at the same time seeking to maintain academic standards. The American system is becoming more committed to the pursuit of excellence whilst seeking to maintain its equalitarianism. These changes in values and institutional forms affect the context in which the teacher must perform his role. It must be pointed out, however, that these trends, in Britain at least, are not universally welcomed, and we will return to these criticisms at a later stage.

The growing heterogeneity of educational grouping

It has already been pointed out that the changes which are occuring in the organization of English education are in the direction of a greater mixing of children of different abilities and from different social backgrounds. Under the 'drop-out' system (Clark, 1961) of selection which has dominated English education in the past, rigid distinctions have been made between children of different measured abilities and educational attainments at 11, 15, 16, and 18 with the successful proceeding to different forms of education from the unsuccessful. As a result, the selected groups became increasingly more homogeneous at each stage of education in both ability and the acceptance of the values held by their teachers. The role of the teacher has been relative to the sort of group which he taught. The primary school has had a much more heterogeneous clientele than the secondary school, but homogeneity has to some extent been achieved at this level through the device of streaming. But with the spread of comprehensive education, de-streaming, and the zoning of schools to ensure a socially-mixed intake, we see a trend towards heterogeneity within schools and within classes at both the primary and secondary levels. This trend presents the teacher with a new set of problems. Firstly, the task of organizing instruction is more difficult in heterogeneous groups than in homogeneous groups. Secondly, many more teachers are going to have to face the problem of motivating children from culturally-impoverished backgrounds.

The movement towards greater heterogeneity has received considerable support from sociological research which has shown how in the past the school which the child attended was to some degree related to the social class position of his parents and also determined the type of education which he would eventually enter (Banks, 1955; Floud and Halsey, 1961; Taylor, 1963). The wastage of ability which thereby occurred has been demonstrated in the Crowther and Robbins Reports as well as elsewhere. Extensive studies have been carried out in this country to indicate social differences in school achievement (Floud, Halsey and Martin, 1958; Fraser, 1959; Douglas, 1964) and the possible determinants of these (Bernstein, 1961; Swift, 1967). A lengthy review of this evidence is not possible here, but the important point brought out by this research is that the child's capacity to profit from education is to an important degree determined by his social environment before he goes to school, and that these differences are often reinforced by the school itself.

It has become clear that those who succeed in our sort of society tend to have internalized a particular set

23

of values. These values include 'future-time' orientation (i.e. an emphasis on future goals rather than on living for the present), 'activism' (i.e. the belief that one can bring about changes in one's condition, as opposed to 'passivism' which assumes that men cannot influence events), and 'individualism' (i.e. an emphasis on individual initiative and a rejection of close relationships with family and kin). These are clearly related to the value of 'achievement' which was discussed above, and they are supported by a particular set of norms which Cohen (1955) has listed as follows: ambition, self-improvement through job, individual responsibility, high valuation on academic achievement, postponement of immediate satisfactions, exercise of forethought, control of aggression, constructive use of leisure, respect for authority, cultivation of courtesy, and respect for property. These are termed 'middle class' norms because they are most firmly held by middle class people, but many working class people also observe these norms—especially if they, or their children, are upwardly mobile. A child who has internalized these norms is more likely to make the best use of his intellectual abilities than a child who has not. He will also meet the 'social' expectations of the teacher and therefore engage the teacher's support in his efforts in school. We thus see once again the possibility of the teacher fusing the two dimensions of 'goodness' and 'cleverness'. Douglas (1964), summarizing his chapter on streaming writes:

> In summary, streaming by ability reinforces the process of social selection which was observed in the earlier chapters of this book. Children who come from well-kept homes and who are themselves clean, well clothed and shod, stand a greater chance of being put in the upper streams than their measured ability would seem to justify. Once there they are likely to stay and improve in performance in succeeding years. This is in striking contrast to the deterioration noticed in those children of similar initial ability who were placed in the lower

streams. In this way the validity of the initial selection appears to be confirmed by the subsequent performance of the children, and an element of rigidity is introduced early into the primary school system.

By virtue of his occupational status the teacher is 'middle class', and he will also hold the middle class norms listed above. For even though he comes from a working class family himself, he will to a great extent have absorbed these norms in the process of his socialization and education. Furthermore it is expected that these will be the norms which he will embody and seek to transmit to his pupils. Thus there will often be a state of 'culture-conflict' between the middle-class teacher and his lower-working-class pupils. The teacher does not understand why the pupil cannot see the importance of 'getting-on'. He fails to recognize very often that 'getting on' means 'getting out' i.e. forsaking his family and neighbourhood ties. For his part the lower working class child fails to see the import of his teacher's exhortations, and regards him as being one of 'them' and not one of 'us' and therefore as having very little of relevance to say. This problem of teacher and pupil 'talking past each other' will increase in extent with the movement towards greater heterogeneity. The graduate teacher working in the grammar school has taught groups with a high degree of value consensus and could 'cool-out' those working class children who did not accept his values and standards. But as comprehensive education develops, he will come to face the same problems of motivation which the college-trained teacher has faced in the secondary modern school. Jean Floud has pointed out that all teachers need to develop a greater awareness of the sociological dimensions of their task (Floud, 1962). She also points out that there is a need for the college-trained teacher to become more aware of the intellectual dimensions of his task. She thus sees the need for a convergence in professional preparation of graduates and non-graduates—which has

hitherto been very different—to meet the needs of an educational system which itself is experiencing a convergence.

An awareness of the sociological dimensions of the teaching task implies that the teacher needs to become aware not only of the social handicaps to learning, but also of the educational implications of retaining an 'ascriptive' orientation towards pupils. The reorganization of the educational system can lead to effective improvements only if it is accompanied by the adoption by teachers of a position which Karl Mannheim called 'pedagogical optimism' which accepts no level of achievement as final. The rather inconclusive evidence on the beneficial effects of de-streaming should not only lead us to question this method of organization as such. The results may be partly affected by the fact that in the large number of schools which have been studied, no distinction has been made between those in which there was a genuine reorientation in staff thinking and a careful planning of the change itself, and those in which the reorganization has not been accompanied by a shift in attitudes.

It has been implied that teachers must seek to encourage the acceptance of the value of achievement amongst all its pupils if levels of educability are to be improved, but two important qualifications must be made. The first is that insofar as the teacher is successful in getting working class children to acquire middle class values, there will still be those who will not accept these values and whose school achievement remains low, and failure will become increasingly harder to bear. As Bernstein (1961) has put it:

> Democratization of the means of education, together with the internalization of the achievement ethic by members of working class strata, may lead to an individualizing of failure, to a loss of self-respect, which in turn modifies an individual's attitude both to his group and to the demands made on him by society.

It has been suggested by Cohen (1955) that in American society at least there is a relationship between delinquency and the inability to achieve success at school. This would suggest that alternative forms of achievement are required and that the 'structure of competition' should be altered (Coleman, 1961). Such a change would present a considerable challenge to the teacher whose major yardstick has been that of *academic* achievement.

The second point is that although certain middle class norms are those which are most closely related to success in our sort of society, working class norms of spontaneity, solidarity and mutual help have their own value. The most difficult task of the teacher is to encourage high motivation amongst working class children without at the same time encouraging a wholly individualistic and 'rat race' attitude to life.

Conflicting values and the teacher as model

Although the problems generated by the growing predominance of the value of academic achievement are most important, these are perhaps less *directly* felt by teachers than some problems arising from other value conflicts. The process of socialization is concerned with the inculcation of values and norms, and most teachers would see their major problems as being in the area of moral education. Emile Durkheim, one of the founding fathers of the sociology of education, saw education as the institution mainly responsible for the maintenance of moral consensus in a secular society (1961). He held that the teacher should embody the central values of society and ensure their acceptance in his pupils—by coercion if necessary. But there is an assumption that there is an easily recognizable core of values which the teacher can transmit. In fact, modern societies are perhaps characterized less by a consensus of values than by a conflict between values. A wide variety of moral, political and religious beliefs are 'available' and this variety presents the teacher with many dilemmas. It would not be appropriate at this point to examine the criteria according to which the teacher can evaluate these beliefs as this is essentially a philosophical question (Peters, 1966), but we can point to some of the conflicts which beset the teacher in his role as 'model'.

Political values. In a totalitarian society the teacher is expected to transmit the official ideology. A conflict will occur where a teacher rejects this ideology, but it is more likely to occur when a teacher's interpretation of an ideology e.g. Marxism-Leninism, deviates from the prevailing 'official' interpretation. In Britain the problem is more complex. There is perhaps a general expectation that the teacher will inculcate democratic values, but in spite of the appeal made during the last war by such writers as Karl Mannheim and Sir Fred Clarke for an explicit formulation of a democratic ideology which the teacher could transmit to his pupils, no such formulation has taken place. It is perhaps true to say that the values which the British school seeks to transmit are class-determined rather than politically-determined. Although there are no pressures upon teachers to eschew membership of political parties—except those of the extreme right and left wings—they are expected to avoid introducing political opinions into their school work. This imposes some strain upon teachers for whom political convictions are part of a more general set of attitudes towards institutions and events including the functions of education. Objectivity is perhaps most difficult to attain where a teacher is concerned with history, social studies, current affairs and similar 'sensitive' areas. It is a mark either of the low level of political consciousness amongst teachers, or their skill in solving their role conflicts, that so few problems arise in this area in Britain. There appears to be a tacit acceptance that schools are agencies of conservation rather than of change, and radical teachers tend to work outside the schools to secure the reorganization of educational institutions which at least provide opportunities for changing values.

Religious values. Conflicts in the area of religion probably trouble British teachers more than conflicts in the area of politics. To what extent the dominant values in British society have evolved from the values expressed in Christian teaching is a most difficult question since they have inspired both radicals and conservatives. There is, however, a widespread belief that Christian values should inform all teaching, and, of course, Christian teaching is given to all children whose parents do not deliberately withdraw them from R.E. lessons and morning assembly. Conflicts are generated for both the Christian and the agnostic teacher. Many Christian teachers who are directly involved in religious education find that the Agreed Syllabus, the purpose of which is to prevent the inculcation of the beliefs of a particular denomination, limits their effectiveness. The teaching of Christianity as a body of historical knowledge coupled with a highly generalized affirmation of Christianity as a way of life seems unsatisfactory to a convinced member of a particular denomination or sect. The role conflict is even more acute for the agnostic. He must decide whether to participate hypocritically in the religious teaching of the school or to risk opprobrium by withdrawing from assembly and the teaching of religious education. We have no detailed knowledge of the pressures which teachers experience in this sphere, but there is no doubt that the line of least resistance is to conform. The general expectation was given its most official form in a Memorandum issued in 1961 by Lord Eccles when he was the Minister of Education to the effect that a good teacher would be a Christian teacher. It is possible that many teachers resolve the conflict by accepting that Christian teaching embodies the important secular values of British society and that it is worthwhile to transmit these in a Christian form.

Professional values. Conflict is generated when there is a widespread expectation that the teacher will perform his role in a manner which is contrary to his own professional values of intellectual integrity, free discussion, unrestricted accessibility to knowledge, etc. Although such conflicts occur in Britain, they are particularly acute for the American teacher who, for example, even up until 1967 was in some states prevented from teaching the theory of evolution since this was held in conflict with the beliefs which he was expected in inculcate. During the 1950s, and even to some extent today, the American teacher has had to face a conflict between a belief in the free pursuit of knowledge and the expectation that he should not teach anything which could be remotely interpeted as being favourable to Communism. This conflict has been particularly acute for teachers of social studies and current affairs. In David Riesman's expression such a teacher 'both draws upon what is in the papers and risks getting into them'. That it is a conflict which did not entirely disappear with the decline of McCarthyism is made clear by a recent case—in Paradise, California —in which an attempt was made to dismiss a woman teacher for a 'liberal' approach to current affairs after one of her pupils had recorded her lessons on a tape which had then been taken by his father to the local school board (Baron, 1964). For a number of historical reasons (Baron and Tropp, 1961), the British teacher has a greater degree of academic freedom and does not face this conflict in a form as acute as his American counterpart. But he does face it to some degree as he seeks to maintain a balance between academic integrity and conveying value judgments which may, in the sensitive areas of religion, politics and sex, be unacceptable to the parents of many of their pupils.

Cultural values. The growing emphasis on the instrumental aspects of education such as its importance for getting a good job, presents the teacher with what is potentially another area of conflict. His professional values may centre upon the subject which he teaches and he will then see his task as one of stimulating in his pupils a love for, say, history, irrespective of its instrumental value. On the other hand, his pupils may for the most part, and in spite of inspired teaching, be mainly interested in passing O level History as one of the six subjects which he has to pass in to get a job of a certain kind or to enter the sixth form. This has, of course, long been a problem for the teacher, but at the present time economic pressures and manpower demands are exacerbating this difficulty, and, some educationists claim, are diverting the teacher away from his true function. G. H. Bantock (1963, 1966), a critic who takes a conservative attitude towards education, maintains that present trends are making it difficult for the teacher to perform effectively his function of transmitting the more conscious part of the culture of his society, and that as a result cultural standards are deteriorating. He is particularly troubled by a possible decline in the cultural standards of the elite as changes in the educational system make it increasingly difficult for the teachers of this group to maintain the standards of the 'high' culture. A radical critic, Raymond Williams (1961), believes that current trends in society and education are preventing the teacher from creating a consensus of shared assumptions amongst all pupils. He sees the role of the teacher as being concerned with the transmission of a 'common culture', but notes that the emphasis on selection and differentiation make 'communality' difficult to achieve. Both radical and conservative critics oppose the drift towards a meritocracy. The conflict for the teacher often comes down to his deciding what is 'good' for the pupil from the viewpoint of the broadest professional values, and what is 'good' for him as an individual seeking a job in a society in need of highly specific skills.

Social pressures affecting the teacher's orientation to his pupils

Economic pressures and manpower demands have come to involve the teacher in the process which has been called 'the bureaucratization of the talent hunt'. Specialization and co-ordination, the two major characteristics of the bureaucratization, have affected the teacher's instructional, selective and socializing roles and hence his orientation towards his pupils. The difficulties which beset the teacher in seeking to reconcile his different roles can be seen as part of a much larger pattern of social relationships. The American sociologist, Talcott Parsons, as part of a general theory of social interaction, has suggested that any individual who is in interaction with another must resolve a certain set of dilemmas before he can act. He called these dilemmas 'pattern variables' and they are of considerable use to us in understanding some of the problems faced by the teacher in an industrialized society (Parsons, 1951).

Affectivity v affective neutrality. This dilemma concerns the emotional tone of a relationship which can be warm (affective) and gratifying to the individual concerned or neutral. The socializing function of the teacher would appear to demand an affective relationship with the pupil since identification would appear to be necessary to the acquisition of values by the pupil. It may also be the case that formal instructions will be more effective when the relationship between teacher and taught is affective, but the specialization and routinization of the teacher's task—which is increasing with the introduction of such techniques as teaching machines and programmed learning —makes an affective relationship more difficult to achieve.

Specificity v diffuseness. This dilemma refers to the extent of the commitment which the role player adopts towards another individual. In our society many roles are specific i.e. the role-player's commitment to the other person is limited. The role of the shop assistant is to serve the customer, the role of the doctor is to cure his patient, but some roles, such as the role of mother, are still diffuse in that they are concerned with a much wider range of functions. The role of the teacher can range from the highly specific to the highly diffuse. It is diffuse when the teacher acts as friend, counsellor, confidante and object of identification. It is specific when the teacher emphasizes his specialized instructional and selective roles. The role of the infant teacher is 'maternal' and is therefore to a large extent diffuse (although it is clear that maternalism is not enough at this stage and that some aspects of the infant teacher's role are specific). At the primary stage the role maintains a high degree of diffuseness, but during the secondary stage of education the role becomes much more limited and specific. Many of the socializing and welfare functions which in the primary school are carried out by the class teacher become in the secondary school much more specialized and carried out by people occupying specific roles such as house-master and year-tutor.

Universalism v particularism. This dilemma is concerned with the way in which one actor judges another. The basis of the judgement is universal when the criteria which are applied to one individual are exactly the same as would be applied to anyone else. Our legal system is founded on the assumption that a judge will deal with all individuals who come before him, whoever or whatever they are, according to the same universal principles. Particularistic judgments, on the other hand, are made according to one's special relationship with the person being judged. Thus the individual will judge his friends, family and perhaps members of the same club, old boys' association or social class according to special criteria. There is in teaching the possibility of adopting either orientation. In a democratic society it is expected that the teacher will judge a child in accordance with some universal criterion such as performance in an examination irrespective of who he is. But there is a dilemma here which can be seen in the evidence of Douglas cited earlier which indicated that teachers tend to favour middle class pupils when allocating children to streams. To favour a child from the middle class—either consciously or unconsciously—is an example of particularism. On the other hand it is often necessary for the teacher to 'make exceptions' and apply particularistic criteria to a child in order to establish a close personal relationship with him and foster his individual development. (A similar dilemma faces the lecturer in a college of education. When supervising a student on school practice he must help him to overcome his teaching problems, but at some point he must stand back and give the student a final teaching mark on the basis of a universal standard.)

Quality v performance. The dilemma is very similar to the preceding one and also to the distinction between 'ascription' and 'achievement' which was made earlier in the chapter. The teacher can orientate towards the pupil on the basis of some quality such as age or sex or on the basis of his educational achievements.

Self-orientation v collectivity orientation. This dilemma is concerned with whether the individual puts his own needs first or the needs of some collectivity to which he belongs. One of the criteria of a profession in our society is that members put the interests of the collectivity before their own interests, and teachers are professionals insofar as they put the interests of the children before their own interests. But there are difficulties here as when a teacher has to decide between the interests of his pupils and his own career opportunities.

Some of the problems arising from these trends have

been discussed by Bryan Wilson in his important article on the role of the teacher (Wilson, 1962). In particular Wilson points out that the trends towards specialization and bureaucratization are encouraging a trend towards greater specificity and neutrality in the teacher's role with a consequent undermining of its socializing functions. He writes:

> Because our society is a society in which specialization continually increases, prestige increasingly attaches to the specialist. But there are distinct limits to the extent of specialization in teaching because the role is diffuse. Again, because our society relies on increasing technologization, it is instrumental roles which win social approval—in which clearly defined operations are undertaken and means are manipulated to achieve proximate ends, which in turn become means to further ends. In some measure increasingly higher rewards are given to those whose roles involve them in the use of elaborate equipment—both technical and organizational. But the teacher's role is not directly instrumental—it is concerned with ends, with values. It is, of its nature, personal and direct.

Conclusion

In an industrialized society, the role of the teacher is open to many pressures and conflicts. These arise from the changing social functions of education which stem from economic and social changes. In particular, the instructional and selective functions of the teacher have grown in importance whilst his socializing function has become more difficult as the teacher's role has become more technical and specialized. Moreover, the heterogeneity of values and beliefs in a complex industrialized society make it difficult for the teacher to act as a 'model' which is appropriate to all his pupils and has the support of their parents.

3

The teacher in the school

In the two preceding chapters the role of the teacher has been discussed in general terms and in relation to society as a whole. The concept of *role*, however, is very complex and highly important for the behavioural sciences. Therefore before proceeding to discuss the role of the teacher in the school, it will be necessary to analyse the concept in a little more detail.

Havighurst and Neugarten (1962) define the concept as follows:

> A social role is defined as a coherent pattern of behaviour common to all persons who fill the same position or place in society and a pattern of behaviour *expected* by other members of society.

The concept thus indicates:

a. a position (or status); *teacher* is a specific occupational position

b. a pattern of behaviour associated with that position; there is a pattern of behaviour associated with the position *teacher* which is independent of any particular person occupying that role

c. a pattern of expectations held of the occupant of a position; the expectations held of a teacher will imply how he ought to act, not merely how it is anticipated that he will act.

The role concept is important because it helps to explain one of the basic characteristics of social life which is that we base our behaviour towards the occupant of a particular role position on the assumption that in general he will tend to conform to expectations and fulfil certain obligations. This is the underlying economy of social life in that in assuming a certain degree of predictability in the behaviour of the occupants of a given role, we need not invest time and energy in seeking to establish role relationships from scratch. When we know that a person is a teacher we will know roughly how he will act when performing his role. When a parent visits a teacher at school in order to discuss the progress of his child, both parent and teacher will have a general notion of the appropriate behaviour of the other and will themselves act according to this (although there are, of course, many modifying factors as, for example, when the parent is himself a teacher).

The teacher will have become aware of some of the expectations of the role whilst he himself was at school. Later, during his training as a teacher, he will have undergone a process of professional socialization in which he will have acquired the behavioural style expected of a teacher and also internalized the values of his profession. To a large extent role behaviour becomes 'second nature', but in many roles there is also an element of premeditation. T. S. Eliot wrote:

> There will be time, there will be time
> To prepare a face to meet the faces that you meet,

and Erving Goffman, a most perceptive writer on the subtleties of role playing has noted that 'roles may not only be *played* but also *played at*'. There is little doubt that the teacher also *plays at* his role. Willard Waller, in his classic study of the sociology of teaching (1932), wrote:

> The teacher must talk to boys of the things in which boys

37

are interested. He must understand adolescent roles, and live vividly roles of his own not wholly incompatible with the roles of adolescence. The persons who are happiest in these roles, and perhaps most successful in playing them, are individuals who have never wholly made the transition from their own adolescence, the college heroes, the football players, the track stars, and the debaters who have never quite forgotten their undergraduate conception of themselves. These persons are able to live adolescent roles vividly because there is no discontinuity in those roles of their own lives. More introspective teachers may resent the parts they have to play. But teachers must always take very seriously the social system designed for the edification and control of children. He must speak seriously and even prayerfully of examinations, grades, credits, promotions, demerits, scoldings, school rituals, making good, etc. And it is difficult for the teacher to take such things seriously and yet keep them from entering his soul. In the main, the better teacher he becomes, the further they will enter.

(When read by student teachers, this passage inevitably evokes two reactions: an apoplectic rejection or a smile which implies 'Others, yes. But not me!' It is rarely accepted as what will happen to oneself. Some reasons for this are suggested in Chapter 5.) Some teachers come to embody *in extremis* some of the qualities expected of the role. This often leads them to be referred to as 'typical teachers' not because they are typical in any statistical sense but because they conform to the exaggerated expectations of the role which we refer to as a stereotype.

Thus the concept of role helps us to understand how expectations help to determine the quality of interpersonal relationships. It also helps us to understand the functions which the teacher performs in the school, the community and in society as a whole. But it is a complex idea and we must make five additional points before we proceed.

The teacher's 'public' is differentiated. Some members of the public will have only the most general expectations of the teacher, but other groups—school governors, inspectors, pupils, parents of pupils etc.—have a much more direct relationship with the teacher and their expectations are therefore much more specific. These groups are known as a 'role set' (Merton, 1956) and their expectations will have a high, although not equal, significance for the teacher.

The teacher's role itself is differentiated according to such criteria as function (subjects and ages taught), authority (over other teachers), attributes (qualifications, experience) and so on. Different expectations are therefore held of different types of teacher.

Individuals have many roles, thus a teacher may also play the roles of father, husband, member of the N.U.T., youth club leader, and captain of a darts team. Different sets of expectations will be held of each role and these might not be compatible. (See below).

The expectations held of an individual occupying a given role may not always be in harmony. When an individual is confronted with different sets of expectations he faces a potential role conflict. Although role conflict takes many forms, three are of particular importance:

i. conflict which occurs because different groups have varying expectations of the same role as when a headmaster, colleagues and parents each have conflicting expectations of the role of a teacher,

ii. conflict which occurs because expectations of two or more roles occupied by one individual e.g. teacher and N.U.T. member, are in conflict,

iii. conflict which occurs when the expectations held of an individual as the occupant of a particular role are incompatible with his personality needs. (See below).

Finally, an important point which will have been troubling the perceptive reader since the beginning of this chapter and which can be expressed in the question: To what extent is the teacher's behaviour determined by the expectations held of him, and to what extent is he free to perform his role according to his own desires? This is a question which cannot be answered here in detail, but it can be pointed out that a teacher is to some extent like *all* other teachers, like *some* other teachers, like *no* other teacher. Expectations prescribe a minimum pattern of behaviour for a teacher the flouting of which would eventually evoke sanctions, but beyond this the teacher has a high degree of autonomy. When an individual becomes a member of some organization such as a school, he must conform to certain expectations if he, and the school, are to function effectively, but at the same time he has the opportunity to fulfil to some degree his unique personality needs. This can be shown diagrammatically in the model of a social system which Getzels and Guba have devised (1957):

NOMOTHETIC DIMENSION

IDIOGRAPHIC DIMENSION

Any action performed by an individual in an organization such as the school is the outcome of his fulfilling his responsibilities to the school and also fulfilling his own personality needs. When both role and personality are fulfilled in the same action, then the individual will experience satisfaction, if they are not then the individual will experience conflict. The teacher has a greater opportunity to play his role according to his own personality needs than, say, a soldier, but less so than an artist.

Spindler (1963) gives the following example of how an American school principal performed his role with considerable efficiency but gave greater rein to his own dispositions than is usual:

> But lest we conclude that personalities and roles must be exactly matched for success to ensue, let it be said that there are some personality types that seem to be able to remake the role to suit their personalities—even the sensitive principal's role. For example, in one school studied in a large metropolitan system the principal was a man in his late thirties who brought an unusually colourful personality to the position. He had a vigorous temper and was not above using four letter words to express it, even in heated arguments with the superintendent and his staff about policy matters, but he was equally inclined to forgive and forget. He was known to drink immoderately at times, but never around students. He liked horse racing and wagered frequently. He wore very unconservative sports coats and drove a low-slung foreign car. He was extremely popular with the majority (though not all) of his faculty, students, and public audiences. Transgressions on the expectations of ordinary propriety (as applied to the school administrator) were forgiven with an almost prideful smile and a 'Well you know Jack!' comment. Other principals viewed him with affectionate lenience and asked each other 'how he got away with it'.... He covered himself concerning the obligations of his professional role and then proceeded to test the limits of the public image connected with the peripheral aspects of this role.

Throughout the remainder of this chapter, we will be less concerned with the personalities of teachers than with the sets of expectations held of different teaching roles within the school by teachers themselves and others.

The basic role of the teacher

In Chapter 2 we looked at some of the fundamental

roles of the teacher from the standpoint of society. In order to see how teachers themselves perceive their basic role, Musgrove and Taylor (1962) asked a sample of teachers working in different types of school to rank six commonly accepted educational aims in the order in which they valued them. The six aims were: moral training, instruction in subjects, social training, education for family life, social advancement and education for citizenship. There were a number of variations between the role perceptions of teachers in different situations which will be discussed later in this chapter, but in general there was an emphasis on instruction and moral training. Social advancement was ranked very low, which suggests that teachers do not see their role as directly promoting social advancement in a direct manner but that they promote it indirectly by emphasizing moral training and instruction and thus promoting both 'goodness' and 'cleverness'. It is clear from this piece of research that the teacher who seeks to 'educate for citizenship' or 'educate for family life' would be deviating considerably from the role expectations of his colleagues.

There is, however, perhaps a more fundamental expectation of the role of the teacher which must be fulfilled by all if they are to be effective. Before any of the broader social roles can be adequately performed, the teacher must be able to control his class. The element of control is fundamental to all sets of expectations concerning the role of the teacher. The notion of 'teacher' amongst the public at large probably evokes the image not of a man marking essays, preparing an experiment or writing a teaching-machine programme, but of a man seeking, with varying degrees of success, to maintain authority over his pupils. Ability to control his class is also basic to the expectations held of a teacher by his colleagues, and from the point of view of the head-teacher a teacher's competence is assessed in the first place upon his ability to maintain order. It will frequently be assumed that he is not an effective teacher unless he keeps his classes under control whatever his success may be in generating spontaneity and creativity in his pupils. A teacher who cannot maintain control is regarded as a threat to the good order of the school as a whole upon which teachers depend to minimize wear and tear on the nerves. There may be a feeling of self-satisfaction amongst some teachers when a colleague cannot keep discipline, and, paradoxically, the presence of a teacher who fails to maintain adequate discipline may reinforce the value of control by forcing all teachers to reconsider their own competences, but if undisciplined behaviour is spilling out of the classroom into the corridors or the rooms of other teachers who have to quell a hurly-burly before they can begin to teach, then the offending teacher's prestige will be very low. This fundamental preoccupation with control generates a wide range of norms through which teachers hope to minimize the spread of indiscipline. These norms include the maintenance of 'social distance' from the pupils and, in public at least, a ceremoniousness in interaction with colleagues. Any undue familiarity with pupils on the part of a teacher is seen as a threat to the general esteem of teachers, with perhaps the additional suspicion that the teacher who is too familiar with his pupils is undermining the authority of his colleagues by talking about them in terms other than reverential. Any undue familiarity between teachers in the presence of pupils is often seen as potentially stripping the teacher of his authority image, hence the reluctance some teachers have of calling colleagues by their first names in the presence of pupils. The injunction on the staff-room door: 'Knock and wait' is partly to prevent the teacher from being seen in an informal and relaxed state by a pupil. Willard Waller (1932) has pointed out that even in a progressive educational establishment, the teacher's effectiveness is dependent upon being recognized as an authority figure. He writes:

The teacher-pupil relationship is a form of institutionalized dominance and subordination. Teacher and pupil confront each other with an original conflict of desires, and however much that conflict might be reduced in amount, or however much it may be hidden, it still remains. The teacher represents the adult group, ever the enemy of the spontaneous life of groups of children. The teacher represents the formal curriculum, and his interest is in imposing the curriculum upon children in the form of tasks; pupils are much more interested in their own world than in the dessicated bits of adult life which teachers have to offer. The teacher represents the established social order in the school, and his interest is in maintaining that order, whereas pupils have only a negative interest in that superstructure. Teacher and pupil confront each other with attitudes from which the underlying hostility can never be altogether removed. Pupils are the material in which teachers are supposed to produce results. Pupils are human beings striving to realize themselves in their own spontaneous manner, striving to produce their own results in their own way; insofar as the aims of either are realized, it is at the sacrifice of the aims of the other.

This highly provocative passage written, it must be remembered in 1932, would be questioned by many teachers and not only those in such progressive private schools as Summerhill. But it does serve to make the point that current expectations of teacher and pupil roles tend to embody assumptions of hostility even though of a very mild sort. Only a complete redefinition of both roles could possibly remove this hostility altogether. At present, the ideology of control is supported by a wide range of staffroom norms. Beginning teachers are almost inevitably advised to forget the kid-glove techniques which they were taught at college and to get a firm grip on the pupils. They will also learn that it is not considered appropriate to talk too much or too enthusiastically about their pupils, and they will hear remarks such as: 'Oh, well! I'd better go and sort out that 2C shower' as experienced teachers go off to their various classes. In many schools there is a discrepancy between such remarks and the actual attitude of the teachers to the pupils, but they do serve to underline the general concern with control. In some schools, however, the teacher-pupil conflict is real and on the pupils' side goes beyond the natural exuberance of youth. Webb (1962) has given an account of how the control ideology is perpetuated in a tough secondary modern school:

> Now let us turn to the teacher's side, making the best possible assumption about the new teacher—that he comes in full of idealism and energy. Secretly he despises his colleagues. He will never be a drill sergeant as they are. In class he tries to be relaxed, treats the lads as equals. This does not work because they play him up. He is a chink in the armour of the system which oppresses them. At first he looks upon fighting for control as a game. So do the boys. Then he begins to get tired. There is ridicule from his colleagues. The head seems to be saying good morning rather coldly. A game's a game, the new teacher thinks, but the 'blighters' don't seem to know when to stop. And he has not enough energy left at the end of the day to do anything worthwhile. After spending the first weeks of the holiday in bed, he resolves to do as a kindly colleague advises—to 'really get on top of the blighters next term from the word go'. In a year or so, if he is not qualified to move, he is another drill sergeant. Thus Black School perpetuates itself.

This presents the extreme case and in the great majority of schools the problem of control is not as serious as this. But it does serve to emphasize the point which is often omitted from educational discussion which is that expectations regarding control and expectations regarding pupil freedom are not always easily reconciled.

The role of the headteacher

For a variety of historical reasons the role of the British

45

headteacher is by far the most significant in the school, and an incumbent of this role probably has a higher degree of power and authority than his counterpart in other societies (Baron, 1956; Stones, 1963; Westwood, 1966). In the absence of research on the role of the headteacher in this country, we can draw a number of inferences from studies of the role of the American school principal.

The first point that can be made is that there is an expectation that the headteacher will be a leader rather than an administrator in the narrowest sense of that term i.e., he will be an innovator with regard to the goals of the school and will not merely concern himself with keeping the school ticking over. It appears that as with leaders in all situations, the headmaster must seek to perform two basic functions: he must be 'task oriented' i.e. he must establish and seek to fulfil certain goals, and he must also be 'person oriented' i.e. he must try to meet the personal needs of members of his staff. In the terminology of Getzels and Guba he must seek to reconcile the idiographic and nomothetic dimension of the school. In the terminology of Hemphill and Coons (1957) he must reconcile the dimensions of *initiating structure* and *consideration*. Initiating structure concerns the formal relationship which the head has with his staff. The head who scores high on this dimension makes his attitudes clear to the staff, criticises poor work, maintains definite standards of performance, asks staff members to follow standard rules and regulations, etc. Consideration concerns the informal relationships which the head has with his staff. The head who scores high on this dimension does personal favours for staff members, finds time to listen to them, puts their suggestions into operation, gets their approval on important matters before going ahead, etc. The leadership style of the head has an important impact upon the climate of the school, and Halpin (1966), following on from the work of Hemphill and others, devised scales for studying school climates. Six types of climate emerged to which they gave the names open, autonomous, controlled, familiar, paternal and closed. These climates cannot be discussed in detail here, but we can give a brief description of the 'open' climate i.e. what Halpin regarded as the 'good' climate (Halpin, 1966). It is characterized by teachers who work well together, enjoy friendly relations without feeling the need for a high degree of intimacy, and possess the incentive to work things out and to keep the organization 'moving'. The head sets an example by working hard himself, criticizing or helping teachers depending on circumstances. He shows compassion in satisfying the social needs of teachers, sets up rules and regulations but is also flexible, and allows leadership acts to emerge from teachers.

Although this research was carried out in American schools, the climates described appear to ring true for British schools. There is no doubt, however, that the climate of the British school is to a large extent shaped by the manner in which the headteacher perceives and performs his role. And as secondary schools increase in size and complexity of organization, there will be a challenge to many British heads to reassess their role since the character of a school can change quite radically as it increases in size, and former patterns of leadership become inappropriate. He will need to reconsider the decision-making structure and the communication pattern of his school and whether the way in which he allocates roles and facilities (classes, rooms, equipment etc.) are influenced by professional considerations. These factors are equally important in a small school. When the primary school head spends a sleepless night trying to decide whether Miss Black should take the scholarship class for the fifteenth consecutive year or whether he should allocate it to the young and enthusiastic Mr. White, he is concerned with trying to reconcile his nomothetic and idiographic functions. In view of the complexity of the leadership role of the headteacher, it is rather ironical that we give him little or no training for it. In view of the fact that we are now accumulating research evidence on school administration, there is now a good case for preparing heads for their role in a much less haphazard way than in the past (Taylor, 1966).

Before leaving the role of the headteacher, we can look at some of the expectations which are held of him by teachers. In a study carried out in Chicago (Becker, 1962) it was shown that although teachers accepted the authority of the head—no matter how inadequately he fulfilled his duties—they held certain expectations of him which he had to fulfil in order to retain their support. The most important of these was that the headteacher would 'back them up' against pupils and parents. It was felt that although the teacher had made a mistake and was in the wrong, it was essential for the head to support him even though he might later discipline him. But, as Becker points out, not all heads lived up to this expectation. The failure to support the teacher is attributed to 'cowardice, "liberalism", or an unfortunate ability to see both sides of the question.' These teachers reported that the climate of the school and the ease of maintaining control was directly related to the strictness of the headteacher, and the head who could minimize control—especially in a lower class district—was held in high esteem. A similar set of expectations would appear to apply to the headteacher in this country and they clearly present the teacher with a role conflict. His 'unfortunate ability to see both sides of a question' may result in him having to refuse to support a teacher. In George Orwell's novel *Burmese Days* the British memsahibs would send a recalcitrant native servant to the police station bearing a note which read: 'Please give the bearer thirty lashes'. A similar situation often arises in schools when an exasperated teacher sends a boy to the head teacher with a note reading: 'I want this boy caned!' Refusal to comply with this injunction after an enquiry into the circumstances of the case results in the headteacher being regarded as 'soft'. Margaret Phillips (1965) has suggested that the headteacher, having lost the close relationship with children which he enjoyed as a class teacher (but also the more immediate problems of control), adopts a 'grand-parent' role which is traditionally more indulgent than the role of the parent who, like the class teacher, has the ultimate responsibility of control. The term likely to be used in the staffroom to refer to the head who is regarded as over-indulgent is 'an old Dutch uncle', a somewhat derogatory epithet to imply weakness. We thus see again the degree to which the teacher in the classroom regards control as a basic issue and to which other professional judgements remain secondary.

Specialist roles in the school

Within the school teachers are differentiated in a number of ways and this gives rise to variations on the expectations applied to them. There is a differentiation according to authority. Other authority roles in the school apart from the headteacher are the deputy head, the head of a division of a school e.g. lower school, the housemaster, and the head of an academic department. With regard to their relationship with other teachers, we can surmise that they face, but to a lesser degree, the leadership problems faced by the head. Another basis of differentiation, both between and within schools, is the age of the pupils taught. The older the children taught the more will the expectation shift from regarding the teacher as socializing agent to regarding him as an instructor. The concept of the infant school teacher as a mother figure is an appropriate one since one of her main tasks is to wean the child away from its psychological dependence upon the home and the break must not be too sharp. But it also has its disadvantages in that it sometimes implies that maternalism is enough, but of course this is far from the truth. Headmistresses of girls' schools

49

often write references for girls applying to colleges of education which contain such phrases as: 'Miss Wood is a very nice girl; not very bright, but would make an excellent infant teacher.' Even within the teaching profession, the intellectual competences required of an infant teacher are not fully recognized. At the secondary school level there is a conception of the teacher as subject specialist which has always been the typical role in public and grammar schools and developed in elementary schools at the senior levels between the two world wars to accelerate in the secondary modern school after the 1944 Education Act. This trend has probably been beneficial on the whole. The teacher who specializes in one subject is likely to acquire a professional concern with curriculum developments in that subject through reading about the subject, attending courses and joining such professional organizations as the National Association of Teachers of English or the Physical Education Association. But there are dangers in this conception of the teacher's role. One is that the subject-centred specialist may become too academic and remote from his pupils. Another is that the more diffuse socializing role of the teacher may be de-emphasized, as feared by Wilson (1962). It is unlikely, however, that there will be a return to class teaching from subject specialization, and problems of socialization are, paradoxically, being faced by new specialized roles such as counsellor, tutor, and teacher-social worker.

It appears likely that the actual subject which a specialist teaches may influence the expectations held of him by colleagues and pupils and his own perceptions of the teacher's role which affect his teaching style. Psychological characteristics could well attract teachers to certain subjects, but these are then reinforced by the expectations attached to the role. In an interesting article on the role of the P.E. teacher in the girls' secondary school, Cannon (1964) points out that the fact that she has been socially and geographically isolated during her training and is physically isolated from her colleagues in school through spending much of her time in the gym, on the playing field and in her changing room, limits her 'self-image'. She remains a 'P.E. teacher' and as such she has an ambivalent status amongst her colleagues whose attitudes will be compounded of disdain (because she is non-academic), envy (because of her youth and health), and affection (because she is regarded as not having fully grown up). These expectations considerably circumscribe her role, but, as Cannon points out, even within these limits she performs at least five functions: nurse and medical auxiliary, promoter of positive physical and mental health, skilled performer and coach, organizer of the movement of numbers of pupils, and, in some schools, an aesthetic function through dance.

Professional roles in the school

One of the major characterisitics of a profession is that its members enjoy a high degree of autonomy with regard to their immediate tasks. In the case of the teacher this implies a high degree of personal choice over what and how he teaches. But definitions of a profession are usually based upon medicine and the law in which practitioners work independently, and the professional person working within an organization has to yield some of his autonomy in the interests of co-ordination and the achievement of common goals. Thus the teacher must conform to the imperatives of school organization e.g. the timetable, and also pursue to some extent a common curriculum and levels of attainment (Bidwell, 1965). But the actual degree of autonomy which the teacher can achieve is dependent upon two inter-related factors: administrative relationships within the school, and his own professional orientation. The question of administrative relationships returns us to a consideration of how the headmaster conceives his role. Corwin (1965) has conceptualized two roles within the school; the employee role and the professional role. Expectations of the employee role include the observance of rules determined by superiors, the following of uniform procedures an emphasis on standardized curricula and teaching techniques, and loyalty to the school. Expectations of the professional role, however, include flexibility in handling problems, emphasis on the application of a body of professional knowledge to teaching problems, high teacher autonomy in making decisions regarding curricula and techniques, teacher participation in collective decision-making regarding the goals of the school, and a loyalty to the profession as a whole and its standards. The degree to which the teacher is allowed to develop a professional role within the limits of organizational necessities depends to a large extent upon the head's conceptions of the teacher's role and the sanctions which he is prepared to use to enforce these. The head who establishes only the minimum rules to secure co-ordination but otherwise allows a great deal of autonomy to the teacher is generating an 'open' climate and inducing teachers to regard themselves as professionals. On the other hand, the headteacher who generates a 'closed' climate and hedges his teachers with detailed prescriptions is inducing teachers to regard themselves only as employees. And as we have seen, teachers will tend to conform to expectations.

But the teacher himself will have his own self-conceptions which may persist even when they are contrary to the expectations of the head. An interesting distinction which has been made by Gouldner (1957-8) is between 'cosmopolitans' and 'locals'. A 'local' is a teacher whose loyalty is to the organization in which he works and whose actions are guided by the expectations of those within that organization. The 'cosmopolitan' on the other hand is not so committed to a single organization and his activities are influenced more by fellow professionals outside the school. These two 'latent social roles' and the preponderance of teachers in a school who incline towards one or the other has an important impact upon the climate of the school. The 'local' teacher is perhaps more inclined to adopt the employee role than the more mobile professionally-oriented 'cosmopolitan'.

There is clearly the possibility of conflict between heads and teachers on the definition of the teacher's role. Where this occurs, the teacher is faced with the problem of adaptation. We know little about these patterns of adaptation amongst teachers, but Corwin (1965) summarizes as follows a typology of adaptation amongst American college teachers reported by Page (1951):

> The 'ritualist' frantically obeys all the rules and regulations of the official organization; the 'neurotic' frets about the discrepancy between the rules and actual practices; the 'robber baron' cuts red tape and uses the system for what he feels were its original professional ends; and the 'rebel' disregards all bureaucratic rules.

Presthus (1962) writing about industrial organizations in the main has suggested three other patterns of adaptation. 'Upward mobiles', as the term suggests, accept the *status quo* and earn promotion within the school. The 'indifferent' has no real professional commitment, he goes through the motions of doing his job and finds his personal satisfaction elsewhere. The 'ambivalent' cannot conform to the bureaucratic demands of the school, but is nevertheless professionally orientated and often inspires needed changes. It is a measure of the need for more research that we can say so little about patterns of adaptation amongst school teachers, patterns which have widespread implications for teacher satisfaction and effectiveness.

Informal roles in the school

All organizations have both a formal and an informal structure. In the school the informal structure consists

53

of the unplanned patterns of association between teachers (and of course, amongst pupils). Informal structures have three main functions. Firstly, they allow for individual self-expression in ways not catered for in the formal structure. Secondly, they facilitate the working of the formal organization since no blueprint can prescribe in detail what every individual should do and informal arrangements oil the wheels of the organization. And thirdly they may also seek to modify the official goals and procedures of the formal organization in the interests of the integrity, self-esteem and general ease of the life of the participants.

The workings of the informal structure of a school are very subtle and require very acute observation to grasp them. Hargreaves (1967) has carried out a highly perceptive study of the informal roles of pupils, but only Phillips has reported a study of the informal relationships between teachers. Yet the informal structure of the school is most significant for the individual and for the organization as a whole. Informal roles such as the 'staff-room lawyer', the headmaster's 'nark', and the informal 'social secretary' of the staff play their part in determining the school climate. Iannaconne (1964) has outlined some of the key roles in the informal power structure of a school staff and their functions in controlling the power of the head. But we must again admit that there has been insufficient research on this topic to allow us to make any generalizations about the implications of the informal roles of teachers for the educative process.

Other factors impinging upon the role of the teacher

There are a number of other factors which help to shape the teacher's own conception of his role and the expectations held of him by others. Only a brief mention of some of these is possible here.

Age, sex, qualifications and other attributes of a teacher

will affect both expectations and self-concepts. Qualifications are particularly important. Whether a teacher is a graduate or not is an important determinant of how he is viewed by his colleagues, and, to a lesser extent, by his older pupils. It is perhaps true to say that graduates and non-graduates as groups—and it cannot be emphasized too strongly that many individuals will deviate from the pattern—tend to regard each other with mutual suspicion and often in terms of misleading stereotypes. The graduate tends to regard the non-graduate as having a sound repertoire of teaching techniques acquired during his college course, but as being incapable of teaching his subject up to or beyond O level. The non-graduate will concede that the graduate might have a deeper grasp of his subject, but regards much of this subject knowledge as being irrelevant to the school situation and likely to make the graduate too academic for his pupils. Furthermore, the graduate is not regarded as being likely to possess the basic classroom competences. The non-graduate is often resentful of the fact that the salary structure favours the graduate however incompetent he is as a teacher. There are two patterns of adaptation to these mutual suspicions. One takes the form of compensation in which the graduate conspicuously affirms his classroom competences and the non-graduate his intellectual competences in seeking work at a higher academic level. The other takes the form of exaggeration in which the graduate greatly emphasizes the importance of knowledge of subject and de-emphasizes pedagogical techniques, whereas the non-graduate will emphasize the opposite qualities. In an investigation carried out in Germany, Kob (1961) postulated two major types of self-image amongst teachers. In the case of Type A 'their interpretation of their professional role is not derived from their academic background but is based upon their being teachers; their specific academic training is relative and subordinate to educational functions,' and they hold that 'the ability to teach is based upon outstanding pedagogical skills, whether these are due to training or to particular educational talents'. The self-image of Type B 'is based upon their academic qualifications and their specialized knowledge in certain subjects' and they 'do not feel misplaced in the school or as teachers', but on the contrary, 'sure of their academic superiority, they feel highly competent as teachers, a fact that becomes particularly clear when confronted with colleagues of Type A'.

The type of school in which a teacher works is an important variable. The graduate working in a grammar school will find it easier than the graduate working in a secondary modern school to adopt an 'academic' self-image without any conflict since the whole academic ethos of the school supports this role. Musgrove and Taylor (1965) found that secondary modern school teachers placed more weight upon social objectives in education than their grammar school counterparts. Margaret Mead (1961) has described roles appropriate to different kinds of American school. The teacher in the crowded city school encouraging the child to succeed academically is compared with the 'parent'. The teacher in the 'academy' (perhaps the equivalent of the British grammar or public school) is compared with a 'grandparent':

> The type of teacher who comes closest to this role is the teacher of classics or the teacher who teaches mathematics and science as if they were classics, fixed and immutable, as unchanged and as unchanging as the figures of Keats' Grecian Urn. The gifted teacher of the classics conveys to the child a sense of the roundedness and relatedness of life, of the way in which each period repeats in its own way an old story that has been written in a more gracious and finished way in the past. Any budding desire to explore the new, to make conquests, can be gently, benignly reduced to the expected, by a reference to Diogenes or Alexander.

We can assume that the actual internal organization of the school, helps to shape the way in which the teacher perceives his role. In one American study (Soles, 1964), it was discovered that in a sample of American high schools those which were organized in such a way that each teacher spent a large part of the day teaching a single class were largely 'group oriented' i.e. concerned with the welfare of the members of the class. In contrast, in schools which were organized on the basis of specialization, the teachers were more 'task oriented' and saw themselves as instructors.

The sort of district from which the school draws its pupils is likely to have an effect upon teachers' self conception of their roles. Musgrove and Taylor (1965) showed that primary school teachers in predominantly middle class areas had a much more restricted view of their role than teachers in predominantly working class areas who tended to be more concerned with broader social objectives.

Conclusion

A teacher's actions are determined partly by his own personality and partly by the expectations which are held of him as a *teacher*. But even within the teaching profession, roles are differentiated according to authority, function, attributes such as age, sex and qualifications, and informal social status. Each of these generates different sets of expectations. Moreover, teachers perform their roles differently according to the type of school in which they teach and the sort of district in which it is situated. The factors which lead to an individual teacher performing his role in a certain way is a question for a psychologist and not a sociologist. The sociologist is concerned with patterns of behaviour amongst groups of people and not with individuals, and in recent years there has been a growing amount on research on the teacher's role which is beginning to explain many of these patterns.

4
The teacher in the classroom

Within his own classroom the teacher enjoys a relatively high degree of privacy and autonomy. He does not work under the constant supervision of a superior and can sustain his privacy through a variety of evasion techniques such as putting illustrations over the windows on the corridor side of his classroom. He has this relatively high degree of autonomy since in English schools syllabuses are rarely set out in great detail, and in any case it is well recognized that teaching cannot consist of following a blueprint. This privacy and autonomy thus enables the teacher to enjoy a considerable degree of discretion over what he teaches and how he teaches, and permits him to play a unique set of variations upon the basic teacher role. Within the classroom constraint arises from the nature of the class as a social group. It could happen that the way in which a teacher would prefer to enact his role would be inappropriate in a particular setting. In the case of a new teacher in Black School, described by Webb (1962) and referred to in the preceding chapter, his personality and training might incline him to see his role in democratic and relatively permissive terms, but the qualities of the classes he had to teach might lead him to modify this self-conception.

The way in which a teacher performs his classroom

58

role is dependent upon the external factors discussed in the preceding chapters, the teaching situation itself, and the personality of the teacher himself. It is thus a many-faceted role, and in this chapter we will consider three particular aspects: the sub-roles of the teacher, teaching as leadership, and teaching styles.

The sub-roles of teachers

In the classroom the teacher has two basic sets of roles to fulfil. One set corresponds with the major functions of instruction, socialization, and evaluation. The second set is concerned with motivating pupils, maintaining control, and generally creating an environment for learning. We can call these 'facilitating roles'. These two sets of roles are sometimes performed independently as when a teacher, on entering a noisy classroom, performs a facilitating role in securing silence before proceeding to perform his instructional role. But the two sets are not always so easily distinguished, nor does the teacher think of them as being separate. Inside the classroom he performs a set of sub-roles any one of which might involve the simultaneous fulfilment of a number of functions. They are responses to a total teaching situation. Some teachers play only a very limited range of sub-roles whilst others, depending upon their personality characteristics and their perception of the teaching task, will play a wider variety. There has been insufficient research carried out on the teacher's classroom behaviour to enable us to present an exhaustive list of sub-roles, but Redl and Wattenberg (1951) mention all the more important ones. Each sub-role is accompanied by a brief indication of its function:

a. Representative of society (Inculcates moral precepts).
b. Judge (Gives marks and ratings).
c. Resource (Possesses knowledge and skills).
d. Helper (Provides guidance for pupil difficulties).

    e. Referee (Settles disputes amongst pupils).

    f. Detective (Discovers rule-breakers).

    g. Object of identification (Possesses traits which children imitate).

    h. Limiter of anxiety (Helps children to control impulses).

    i. Ego-supporter (Helps children to have confidence in themselves).

    j. Group leader (Establishes the climate of the group).

    k. Parent surrogate (Acts as object of bids for attention from younger children).

    l. Target for hostilities (Acts as object of aggression arising from frustrations created by adults).

    m. Friend and confidante (Establishes warm relationship with children and shares confidences).

    n. Object of affection. (Meets the psychological needs of children).

It will be noted that with the single exception of Judge —which corresponds to the evaluation function—the three basic roles of the teacher discussed in Chapter 2 are further differentiated largely from the standpoint of pupil-teacher interaction. It will also be noticed that the functional roles and facilitating roles may both be present in a single sub-role; the sub-role of Group Leader, for example, may be performed for both instructional and facilitating purposes. A further point is that the list is relative to American culture, and it may be that the sub-roles of European teachers are less child-centred.

The leadership roles of teachers

A useful way of conceptualizing the role of the teacher is to regard him as a leader. His main task is to lead his pupils towards those learning and behavioural goals which have been prescribed for them or upon which he himself has decided. He will often have to carry out his task in the face of pupil indifference or even hostility, and in order to overcome the reluctance of children to work hard or behave in a manner acceptable to adults, the teacher must develop a variety of leadership techniques which, taken together, constitute a leadership style. There has been a considerable amount of research into the relationship between leadership style and group climate by Lippitt and White, Anderson, Bush, Flanders and others. It is not essential to summarize this research here and the reader is referred to one of the many summaries of this work which do exist e.g. Bidwell (1965), Flanders (1960), Gordon (1964) and Evans (1962). But it is necessary to discuss two important points which arise out of this research.

The first point is that the appropriateness of leadership behaviour in the classroom is relative to the nature of the group and to the task in hand. There are variations between school classes in terms of age, sex, social class background, ability and peer group affiliations, and the teacher's leadership behaviour must take account of these differences e.g. the more 'maternal' role of the teacher of young children would be inappropriate in a secondary school. But a more difficult leadership problem arises from the differences in ability, background, etc. which occur within the same school class—a point previously discussed in Chapter 2. A teacher may develop a leadership style which is appropriate to some pupils in his class—say the children from 'respectable' homes who have acquired a respect for authority, acceptable levels of courtesy, and a certain docility (Henry, 1955)—but inappropriate to other pupils from 'rough' homes who have not acquired the same set of norms. Different teaching functions too require variations in leadership style. Socialization and instruction, for example, require different styles, and Bryan Wilson (1962) has suggested that social forces are creating pressures towards an 'instrumental' leadership role which is inappropriate to the socializing functions of the teacher, and has hinted that this trend might well be a factor in the growth of delinquency (Wilson, 1966). Some tasks require the teacher to take the centre of the stage directing the activities of pupils and controlling their behaviour, whilst other tasks may require the teacher to move from the centre to the periphery and merely create the right conditions for pupil-initiated activities and self-direction. More than one style may be required in a single lesson. The same is true of the different authority patterns of teachers. One of the fundamental problems of the teacher is the involvement-detachment dilemma i.e. how a teacher can become personally involved with his pupils and reduce the social distance between them in order to motivate them whilst at the same time retaining his authority. Waller (1932) distinguishes between the 'institutionalized' leadership behaviour of the teacher which is founded upon the formal supports of the teacher's office, and 'personal leadership' which is based upon the teacher's personal qualities. Waller believed teachers to be too dependent upon the formal trappings of authority and, by and large, missing the opportunity of freer communication with their pupils. But whilst it can be agreed that leadership based upon personal qualities might be the most appropriate form for education, it must also be recognized that there are often adverse situations in schools in which teachers will have to strive for personal leadership from the more secure base of the various forms of institutionalized leadership.

The second point, which follows from the above, is that since no single type of leadership behaviour is appropriate at all times, the successful teacher will be highly adaptable in his behaviour. The skilful teacher can play the role of comedian, kindly uncle, confidante, or any other informal role, but yet retain the capacity to return with ease to a more detached role when necessary without losing the goodwill of his pupils. A less accomplished teacher may play his informal roles successfully, but then have difficulty in reasserting his authority and lose the goodwill which he has generated by becoming aggressive in his struggle to retain control.

The good teacher, as Waller put it in a characteristically telling phrase, 'lengthens and shortens the rubber band of social distance with consummate art'. Cunningham and her associates (1951) concluded from their studies of leadership patterns in the classroom that: 'Teachers whom observers agreed were most effective used the widest range of patterns, according to the appropriateness of the pattern to the situation'.

Studies of what makes a 'good' teacher have, on the whole, been unsatisfactory in that they have tended to look for universal qualities of personality which would characterize the good teacher and ignore the nature of the teaching situation itself. But undoubtedly one of the major qualities of the successful teacher is flexibility. Getzels and Thelen (1960), in applying the social system model of Getzels and Guba discussed in Chapter 3 to the classroom situation, claimed that in some situations (a spelling lesson) the teacher's style would be largely nomothetic whilst in others (an art lesson) it would tend to be more idiographic. They claimed that the successful teacher would develop a 'transactional style' which would draw towards one dimension or the other according to circumstances. We might say that the successful teacher is one who:

a. has the skill to form accurate perceptions of the classroom situation and the changes which occur within this situation,

b. is aware of the teacher roles which are appropriate to different situations,

c. possesses the personality skills which allow him to adapt to changing situations.

Teaching styles

Teachers face a common set of basic problems in the classroom, but the ways in which they seek to solve these vary considerably. The leadership styles of teachers have particular reference to their managerial roles, but teaching styles embrace more than this. The term 'role' refers, of course, to the part which an actor plays, and the dramatic connotation is present in the sociological use of the term. Certain occupational roles demand that the incumbents, in order to enhance their effectiveness, pay some attention to what Goffman has called 'the presentation of self'. The doctor develops his bedside manner, the clergyman his pulpit voice, and the teacher too must bring a dramatic quality to his role in order to stimulate the pupils' interest in himself and thence in the material which he is seeking to teach. Having few effective coercive sanctions at his disposal, he needs to rely upon dramatic stratagems (and many excellent teachers would be most embarrassed if other adults had been secretly observing them 'hamming' it in front of a class). As Waller pointed out he must appear to attach a greater importance to school events than they warrant. He must appear to be committed to minor rules and the maintenance of good order. When a form collapses at school dinner sending four boys sprawling on the floor, and the rest of the school look immediately from the upset to the duty-master to see if there is any tell-tale sign of mirth around the mouth, the teacher will feel that he must remain unamused. In the classroom the teacher will simulate great anger at some youthful pecca-dillo in order to forestall any real breaches of order. With most teachers this act becomes part of their natural behaviour. It is not insincere, certainly it is no more insincere than the histrionics of the barrister who seeks to gain a favourable verdict for his client, and the pupils themselves happily participate in the act. This has long been recognized, and Goldsmith expressed it well in his description of the schoolmaster of Auburn in *The Deserted Village:*

> A man severe he was, and stern to view;
> I knew him well, and every truant knew;

Well had the boding tremblers learnt to trace
The day's disasters in his morning face;
Full well they laughed, with counterfeited glee,
At all his jokes, for many a joke had he;
Full well the busy whisper, circling round,
Conveyed the dismal tidings when he frown'd.
Yet he was kind : or if severe in aught,
The love he bore to learning was in fault. . . .

It will be noted that the glee was 'counterfeited', but the children take pleasure in the fact that to laugh at the schoolmaster's weak jokes was itself a joke which all shared.

In the classroom the teacher acts in accordance with his own image of how a teacher should act. These self-images are dependent partly upon the teacher's personality and partly upon his experience as a pupil, student of education and as a beginning teacher. There thus develops a great variation in teaching styles. Thelen (1954) writes, 'It is as if he had a model in his mind and operated consistently to make the classroom conform to this model; it represents the teacher's idea of what the classroom should be like.'

The global style of a teacher is not easily caught by the usual research techniques and can often be more meaningfully presented in metaphorical terms. Thelen presents seven models of teaching style (Socratic discussion, town meeting, apprenticeship, boss-employee relationship, the business deal, the good old team, and the guided tour) and discusses the potential effectiveness of each of these styles (See also Havighurst and Neugarten 1962). Another model might be based upon a family-relationship metaphor:

Teacher as father. This is a highly instrumental style of teaching. The teacher knows what has to be done and pursues his task in the most efficient manner. There is one 'right' way and the rules and drills must be observed.

65

The teacher is kind and has an interest in all the members of his 'family', but he is not sentimental and permits no nonsense.

Teacher as grandfather. This teacher is good and wise and knows many things, and he is pleased and anxious to pass on his knowledge. He is a teller of tales and his pupils can learn a lot from him if they listen. But, much to his surprise and disappointment, they are not always prepared to listen to him and they often take advantage of his indulgent ways.

Teacher as elder brother. The emphasis here is on doing things together and sharing experiences. The approach is highly practical. The pupil is shown how to do things and then encouraged to try them himself getting practical help when he meets difficulties. The teacher enjoys a great deal of satisfaction from working closely with his pupils, but finds failure highly frustrating.

The teacher as uncle. Here the teacher is like the uncle who has 'been away' and returned with much interesting information and many ideas which he is anxious to pass on to his pupils. Because he is so lively and keeps them interested, the pupils like him and work well. There is little problem of control, because he keeps them involved as he moves from one field of interest to another, and an expression of disappointment is usually an adequate sanction against recalcitrant pupils.

The teacher as cousin. The image here is of a rather wayward cousin. He has much to teach his pupils, but he is not greatly interested in them and his mind is usually on other matters—often on his own career. On the occasions when his interest is roused he is a very stimulating teacher, but for long periods he is simply going through the motions, and the lack of response from his pupils is attributed to their lack of ability or their failure to recognise the special sort of person that he thinks he is.

Teaching styles differ in terms of approaches to material as well as to pupils. An amusing and suggestive typology of teaching styles amongst teachers of English has been suggested by Wilkinson (1966):

The teacher as Grendel's mother. The teacher acts as the guardian of 'the heritage of literature'.

The teacher as sergeant major. The teacher conceives of English as a discipline and uses exercises from such textbooks as *English on Parade* and *Keep Fit Exercises in English*.

The teacher as Sigmund Freud. The teacher uses composition as a means of releasing conflict and tension.

The teacher as group psychotherapist. The teacher uses drama as therapy.

The teacher as printer's reader. The teacher regards a piece of written work as a proof to be corrected.

The teacher as 'teacher'. The teacher plays a routine role teaching 'facts' and avoiding 'frills'. He likes grammar and his own seat in the staffroom.

Although teaching style is a wider concept than leadership style, the point which was made about the latter—that successful teaching probably requires a 'transactional' approach—applies also to the former. Although each teacher will work out his own distinctive style which will inevitably embody his own personality characteristics, a reliance upon one single approach at all times is possibly less fruitful than the ability to ring the changes in accordance with particular situations.

Conclusion

The roles which teachers play in the classroom and the teaching styles which they adopt are greatly varied. Some teachers will have a much more limited repertoire than others, and the teacher's role behaviour will be determined by the nature of his personality, his experiences, and the teaching situations in which he finds himself. If a teacher is unable to match his style to the situation, it is likely that he will be ineffective, unhappy or both. The emphasis in this chapter has been on the need for role flexibility. The student-teacher, on entering college, is often disappointed to find that his tutors give him no sure-fire method of coping with all classroom situations. Different teaching situations require different approaches which themselves must be worked out within the framework of the personality skills and attributes of the individual teacher. A knowledge of the concept of role and a familiarity with a variety of teaching styles will help the student to define his own relationship to classes which he has to teach. Careful observation of the role which experienced teachers adopt would help in this respect as would the opportunity of developing self-awareness through role playing free from the hurly-burly of an operational classroom, but current pressures on colleges and schools often make it impossible to arrange this sort of training.

5
The teacher and the public

The teacher has a much wider public than his pupils and colleagues. Outside the school a number of groups have their own expectations of the teacher's role. These groups include the parents of pupils, local councillors and others who have responsibilities for education, the members of various voluntary organizations which take an interest in education, and members of Parent-Teacher Associations. In addition, members of the public at large will have their own conceptions of the teacher. The degree to which these expectations directly impinge upon the teacher and shape his own conception of his role varies from society to society, and it is useful to compare British and American teachers from this point of view.

Teacher and community in Britain and America

The American teacher is much more susceptible to community control than his British counterpart. This applies to what he does as well as what he is as a person. The community seeks to exert control over the teacher both in school and out. There are a number of reasons for this, but basically the difference stems from historical factors which have led to different structures of control.

In America schools were often founded at grass roots level in small communities and the influence of the local community is still very great. In Britain on the other hand, universal elementary education evolved as a national system with a nation-wide salary structure and standard of entry to the profession. The local authorities themselves tend to be large administrative units controlling densely populated urban areas or large counties. As a result, the British teacher tends to be much more removed than his American counterpart from even local centres of administrative control. He is also insulated from parental pressure since he functions on behalf of society as a whole and not simply of the local community. Baron and Tropp (1961), in their interesting discussion of these contrasts have written:

> The essential difference is perhaps to be summed up as follows: whereas in England it is the teacher who represents to the community in which he works 'nationally' accepted values, in America it is the community that interprets to the teacher the task he is to perform.

A further source of insulation for the British teacher is that his education will have removed him from the non-selected mass, and he will have spent far longer in full-time education than the majority of the parents of his pupils. He therefore maintains an intellectual authority over parents, and the confidence which comes from this habit enables him to deal with parents who are his intellectual equals in an authoritative manner. In America, on the other hand, a far higher proportion of parents will have been educated to college level where they are more likely to challenge the authority of the teacher.

The high degree of control which the American small community exerts over all aspects of the lives of its teachers is notorious. The leisure activities of the teacher, especially women teachers, have, in the past, been closely controlled, although these pressures are decreasing with the growing urbanization of American society. In a similar way the local community has been able to control what was taught in the schools. The British teacher on the other hand, experiences very little community control over his professional activities or his leisure pursuits.

Whereas an American Parent Teacher Association acts as a very influential pressure group, the activities of its British counterpart are largely confined to fund-raising through whist drives and other activities, and tend to receive information and advice rather than to give it. The class teacher in Britain has very little contact with the parents of his pupils. He may meet them once a year on Open Nights, but otherwise any contacts which they have with school will be through the headmaster. It is not unknown for there to be a white line painted across the entrance to a school with the legend: 'No parent is allowed to cross this line without permission' painted above it. Thus although the British teacher is insulated to a large extent from the interference of parents with his professional activities, he is, conversely, unable to have a great deal of influence on them. The actual desire for greater contact with teachers very much depends upon the catchment areas of the school. In the Liverpool dockland area described by Kerr (1958) teachers were regarded along with policemen and social workers as interfering busybodies. Middle-class parents, on the other hand, concerned with the upward social mobility of their children are more likely to want closer contacts with the school. Jackson and Marsden (1962) reported that working-class parents of grammar school children were very hesitant to visit the school for the purpose of making enquiries about such matters as courses, examination subjects, and university entrance requirements.

Musgrove and Taylor (1965) sought to determine how parents view the role of the teacher and how teachers think parents view their role. The results showed that parents, like the teachers themselves, saw instruction in subjects and moral education as the two most important teaching functions. But teachers reported that parents would rate social advancement very high and moral education very low, although they correctly perceived that parents would rate instruction in subjects high. We might have expected that as American parents tend to have close contact with school than British parents, there would be a more realistic appreciation of the expectations of parents by the teachers. No direct comparisons are possible at the present time, but Biddle and his associates (1961) in their extensive study of the role of the American teacher report that there were shared misconceptions between teachers and parents.

The public image of the teacher

The fact that the term 'typical teacher' retains its currency indicates that there exists a stereotype, or a number of stereotypes, dominating the public image of the sort of person a teacher is. This image may not necessarily be shaken by a close acquaintanceship with teachers who in no way conform to it; he will merely be regarded as an exception and the stereotype will continue to operate. The teacher regarded as untypical by his close associates who are not themselves teachers, will still be regarded in the light of the stereotype by people who do not know him so well. This public image leads to a great deal of resentment amongst teachers, and it is not unknown for them to try to conceal their occupation. (A teacher acquaintance of the writer invariably told his partners at dances that he drove a laundry van for a living!). The teacher appears always to be to some extent a man apart. Havighurst and Neugarten (1962) and others refer to the American teacher as a 'sociological stranger' because he is somehow *in* the community but not *of* it. We would not be fully justified, however, in referring to the British teacher as a 'sociological stranger' since he tends to live away from the school in suburban middle-class areas and associate with people with different occupations. It is perhaps significant that although there have been a number of American studies of the community roles played by teachers in the leisure time, there have been no such studies in Britain. It appears to be assumed that in this respect the teacher does not differ from other middle-class citizens in the extent to which they become involved in church or community affairs.

Nevertheless, the public image of the teacher in Britain is of a pedantic, sober, and morally impeccable person. He is regarded with very mixed feeling by the public at large and even by individuals, respect is mixed with ridicule, fear with affection, and admiration with contempt. This stereotype has an important influence upon the extent to which teaching is regarded as a desirable occupation by potential recruits and upon the self-image of the teacher—which often appears to have a slight touch of apology. It can perhaps be explained by the fact that in a number of ways the teacher is an 'intermediate' status.

The teacher is intermediate between the world of adults and the world of children. This leads to the jibe that the teacher is 'a man amongst boys and a boy amongst men' and the view that the unmarried woman teacher is seeking maternal satisfaction through her pupils (a view which does not yet appear to have been greatly shaken by the fact that women teachers are all too marriageable and that the service would grind to a halt without the return of the married teacher to the classroom). Although there are undoubtedly some teachers who over-identify with their pupils and spend much of their leisure in the company of young people, the majority play a wide variety, perhaps an unusually wide variety, of adult roles. It is perhaps the 'play' element in teaching which gives rise to the 'boy amongst men' jibe, but it is only the fact that the teacher works with children which makes this significant. It does not shape the image of the professional sportsman or the soldier whose peacetime activity is very much given over to playing war games.

The teacher is intermediate between the 'real' world and the 'ideal' world. Waller called the school 'a museum of virtue' indicating that the public regarded it as having the function of transmitting values which were not, in fact, operative in society as a whole. The teacher is regarded as having the function of moral improvement and is thus expected to embody all the virtues. The viewpoint of parents would appear to be as follows: 'Although I do not have these virtues myself, I would nevertheless like my children to have them. It is therefore the job of the school to inculcate them and the role of the teacher to embody them.' The parent's injunction to the child is 'do as I say', but it is expected that the teacher's injunction will be 'do as I do' or even 'be as I am'. It is perhaps also expected that the teacher will represent these virtues out of school as well as in, and this accounts for the ambivalence with which the teacher is regarded. As a paragon of virtue he may be despised if he succeeds but pilloried if he fails, and he can be sure that the press will report in full any misdemeanour on the part of the teacher or any case in which the teacher's affirmation of a principle can be made to look slightly ridiculous.

The role of the teacher is often regarded as being intermediate between the world of work and the world of non-work. As the teacher does not participate in the worlds of industry and commerce he is often not considered to be involved in 'work'. His task is regarded as preparing successive cohorts of children for the world of work. Such a view is not necessarily taken of all 'service' professions—nursing, for example, would not be regarded in the same way—but the official hours and holidays of the teacher, and the fact that he works with children rather than adults contributes strongly to this view. There is, however, some ambivalence in this view of teachers. A mother will often say that one child

74

is 'hard work' and she would not fancy managing a class of forty. Another factor contributing to this view is the common belief that teachers have no skills which are employable in the 'real' world of work. This is expressed in Shaw's notorious epigram: 'Those who can do; those who can't, teach'. There is an assumption that those who go to colleges of education do so because they cannot obtain places in universities. This is not *Bull* entirely without foundation. There is also an assumption that university graduates who enter teaching do so because they cannot find suitable appointments in other professions. This again is not without foundation. Although there is no systematic research which reveals that teaching is a second choice occupation for British graduates, Kob (1961) showed that amongst German university graduates who became teachers there was a high proportion for whom it was a second-choice occupation—even after eliminating from the reckoning those who did not have any highly specific career preferences when they entered universities. And Geer (1966) showed that American undergraduates who took courses in education often did so as an 'insurance' against being unable to enter the professions of their choice. None of this, of course, tells us anything about the effectiveness of such people as teachers.

Kob (1963) has drawn attention to another dimension upon which the teacher's role is intermediate which is between the world of scholarship and the world of non-scholarship. A teacher whose subject is history is a 'teacher of history' and not a historian; they do not, as a rule, write history or do research, and even when they do they would be regarded primarily as a teacher. The university teacher of history, on the other hand, is regarded primarily as a historian rather than as a teacher. There is in this country quite a clear division between teachers in universities and schools. The recruitment of teachers from schools to university posts is, except in departments of education, comparatively rare. The teacher of history in the schools, whatever the quality of his initial degree and his own competence as a historian, will be regarded as a purveyor of other people's ideas. That this will be so for the majority of teachers cannot be denied, but the distinction is an artificial one which could inhibit original thinking amongst teachers to the detriment of the subject as a whole. The more teachers are involved at the growing edges of their disciplines, the more effective one would expect their teaching to be. It is probably true to say that the distinction is more rigid in Britain than in some European countries where school teachers are much closer to their university colleagues. But this itself can lead to difficulties when the academically better qualified teachers seek to maintain their superiority over the less well qualified (Kisiel, 1966).

Teacher-parent relationships

The public image of the teacher in Britain is perhaps of the nature of a stereotype because of the relative lack of contact between the individual teacher and the adult public which to some extent retains a childhood view of teachers and schools. It is as parents of school-age children that the public has the greatest potentiality for interaction with teachers, especially working-class members of the public who will tend not to live in the same districts as teachers. But interaction between parent and teacher is relatively limited. If parents make a private visit to school in connection with their child's behaviour or school progress, they are likely to meet only the headteacher. If they attend some school function such as a concert or a display they will see teachers performing only their official roles for the occasion—often shepherding and controlling children in a manner which confirms the stereotype. And if they attend a parents' evening to discuss their child with the class teacher, they will usually have little more than ten minutes allotted to them.

The role relationship between parent and teacher on the occasions when they do interact is a delicate one and often fraught with ambivalence and potential conflict. The aim of the teacher in such exchanges is to enlist the aid of the parent in supporting his objectives, but this aim is often difficult to achieve because parental conceptions of the teacher's role will vary with such factors as social class and the ability of the child, and the teacher can depend upon little consensus about what he is trying to achieve. The lower working-class parent, if he interacts at all with the teacher, may be deferential, hostile, or even both. He will probably have experienced school failure himself and this will have shaped his own perceptions of schools and teachers. He may well view schools as hostile, forbidding and impermeable institutions and teachers as superordinate, socially-superior, and highly-principled individuals. Whether he reacts with deference or hostility it is difficult for the teacher in such circumstances and in such a short space of time to convey the idea that he is on the side of the child and the family. He may, in fact, adopt a superordinate role and implicitly or explicitly criticize the values and way of life of the family. But even when he seeks to meet the parents more than half way, genuine contact may be inhibited by the very language which he uses since this is likely to be 'formal' rather than 'public' (Bernstein, 1961), and hence convey the impression of social distance. And if his role performance is marked by 'universalistic', 'specific' and 'affectively neutral' orientations, this will have the same effect. His relationship with middle-class parents will be ostensibly much easier insofar as teacher and parents will be 'talking the same language', but there may well be difficulties in this relationship if the middle-class parent regards the teacher as an equal, or less than equal, who has to be in some way manipulated in order to ensure his child's success.

So long as the teacher and the parent are in agreement upon the child's ability, motivation, behaviour, and educational needs, then the relationship may present no problems to the teacher, but where there are implicit or explicit disagreements upon these points, a situation of potential role conflict arises for the teacher. He must determine the degree to which his professional judgements are to take precedence over the wishes, or perhaps even demands, of his 'clients'.

It is probably true to say that on the whole the British teacher has been more concerned to exercise his professional judgement than to heed the wishes of parents. But it is now widely suggested that the teacher cannot fully exercise this judgement without an adequate knowledge of the child's home background, or at least his social milieu. At the present time the expectation that the teacher will extend his role to embrace closer contacts with the home is only weakly held by students of education, lecturers in colleges of education, and headteachers (Finlayson and Cohen, 1967), but there is a growing opinion that teaching should be more closely linked with the home either through the redefinition of the role of all teachers or through the creation of special roles linking the home and the school (H.M.S.O., 1967: Craft, Raynor, and Cohen, 1967). And the view is developing in America that parents ought to be encouraged to play a much more positive role in the educational enterprise through such roles as 'foster teachers' for disadvantaged children, 'teachers-aides' within the school where they would present the views of the community to educators, and members of Parents' Clubs which would organize the social and recreational activities of pupils (e.g. Wilcox, 1967).

Changes of this kind would have a considerable significance for the professional status of the teacher. The professional consults his client and becomes aware of his needs, but then bases his action upon a body of professional knowledge. He is able to retain relative ascendancy over his clients because their knowledge of medicine, law, architecture, etc. is relatively limited and is also assumed to be limited. A closer relationship with the parents of his pupils would enable the teacher to pay greater attention to the particular needs of his clients, but as parents are more likely to assume a knowledge of appropriate teaching methods than of, say, appropriate medical treatment, the teacher must take care to protect his professional independence and affairs the theoretical foundations of his practical skills of which the layman will have little awareness. We turn to the problems of the teacher as a professional person in the next chapter.

Conclusion

The teacher in Great Britain has a relatively high degree of insulation from the local community. This serves to protect him from undue parental pressures, but perhaps also leads to the persistence of certain stereotypes of the teacher which detract from his prestige in the community. There is, however, a growing demand that the teacher should establish closer links with the home in order to become sensitized to the particular problems and needs of his 'clients'. But in establishing these links the teacher's professional role might come under some pressure.

6
Teaching as a profession

The status of the individual teacher, his self-esteem, and the manner in which he performs his role are to some extent dependent upon the status of the teaching profession in society. This is more than simply the question of whether teaching is, in fact, generally referred to as a profession, for it is likely that the majority of people would, if asked, classify it as such (Terrien, 1953). It is a question of whether teaching enjoys, or is likely to enjoy in the future, the prestige and privileges which are accorded in our society to such high status occupations as medicine, law, dentistry, architecture, etc. which are at the top end of the professional continuum. We must, therefore, try to establish the criteria by which an occupation is judged a profession, establish the degree to which teaching meets these criteria, and consider some of the barriers to the professional advancement of teaching.

The criteria of a profession

The first point to note is that the term 'profession' is not a precise *descriptive* concept but more an *evaluative* concept. As Everett Hughes has put it: 'the term profession is a symbol for a desired conception of one's work and hence, of one's self' (Hughes, 1951). Since the most prestigeful occupations are termed professions, the term is symbolic of the status to which less prestigeful occupations aspire. Thus occupations called, or calling themselves, 'professions', can be ranged upon a continuum from those which are universally recognized as such to those, such as hairdressing, which are thus recognized only by a few. Although the quest for a set of criteria by which a profession can be recognized has been proceeding for at least fifty years, no universally acceptable list has been produced. Whilst there is widespread consensus on certain basic criteria, there are also wide variations between the various sets which have been offered (Millerson, 1964). In his important book on teaching as a profession, Lieberman (1956) offers eight criteria not as 'a foolproof set of specifications' but as 'a complex set of characteristics'. The following list of criteria, which are similar to Lieberman's, should also be so regarded.

A profession performs an essential social service. There can be little doubt that education fully meets this criterion. The service which education performs is essential to the individual child who could not be fully socialized in an industrial society if he did not spend a lengthy period in full-time formal education, and to society which depends upon people not only having been socialized but also prepared for occupational roles requiring high degrees of skill.

A profession is founded upon a systematic body of knowledge. The implication here is that a profession is not merely concerned with the exercise of some skill, but a skill which has an intellectual foundation. The intellectual foundations of teaching include both subject-matter knowledge and a knowledge of educational theory. Education differs from other professions in having the subject-matter component, but in many ways the theoretical knowledge needed by the teacher performs the same functions as that needed by the doctor. Both education and medicine are secondary disciplines which are informed by a number of primary disciplines; in the case of medicine these primary disciplines include anatomy, physiology and biology, and in the case of education they include philosophy, sociology and psychology. It would thus appear that education meets this particular criterion of a profession, although some people still deny that there is any body of knowledge called 'education' which is distinct from knowledge of subject matter. And even now in this country a university graduate is *ipso facto* recognized as a qualified teacher without having undergone a period of practical or theoretical training.

A profession requires a lengthy period of academic and practical training. Teaching certainly fulfils this criterion, but the teacher's period of training is not as long as that required for doctors, lawyers, architects and some other professionals. Moreover there remains some uncertainty about the appropriate balance between subject-matter studies, the study of educational theory, and practical work. The graduate taking the certificate in education course spends far less time on the study of the educational theory than the student who has attended a college of education, especially if the latter has taken a B.Ed. degree. On the other hand subject studies in colleges of education are often still regarded as 'teaching' studies rather than as a contribution to personal education.

 A profession has a high degree of autonomy. The notion of professional autonomy covers two different but related factors: the autonomy of the individual prac- titioner to make decisions in the interest of his clients, and the autonomy of the profession as a whole to make decisions about its modes of operation. The individual teacher has some degree of autonomy over the work which he does with his pupils, but it is monitored by headteachers and also to a greater or lesser degree by local inspectors and H.M.I.'s. Whether teachers can be regarded as having high autonomy or not is dependent upon how one defines the term (Elvin, 1963; Morrell, 1963). A further point is that such monitoring of the teacher's work as occurs is carried out largely by other educationalists and not by laymen. Thus to some extent teaching fulfils the criterion of individual autonomy.

A profession as a whole is autonomous if it is self-governed and has ultimate control over its functions. Medicine enjoys self-government through the British Medical Council, and law through the Law Society. These professional associations retain the responsibility of issuing a licence to practise or withdrawing this for incompetence or misconduct. They also have a powerful voice in determining national policy on health and medical or legal matters. Teaching is not a self-governing profession although it has long aspired to this. In 1912 a Teachers' Registration Council was established in an effort to control entry into the profession, but since individuals could practise as teachers without being on the Register, the movement was ineffective and ceased to exist in 1949 (Baron, 1954). And in 1966 when the teachers' unions issued a document proposing a General Teachers' Council which would control entry, the then Minister of Education, Mr Anthony Crosland, stated that in a period of national teacher shortage he could not abrogate his responsibility for teacher supply. Thus entry to teaching and expulsion from teaching remain formally under the control of the Department of Education and Science, but it should also be recognized that *de facto* control in all but a small number of marginal cases remains within the teacher training institutions and hence under the control of educationists, and although laymen may have some say in first appointments and promotions, the headteacher and educational administrators have an important and often crucial, voice.

The question of the autonomy of the teaching profession to determine its own social functions and modes of operation is complex. Insofar as these operations are determined by the *structure* of the educational system clearly authority lies with the government and local authorities and the organized teaching profession acts through its unions only as a pressure group. The *content* of education, however, is not centrally controlled nor locally controlled, although the Schools Council acts as an advisory body and both H.M.I.'s and local inspectors and advisors may seek to convey to teachers national and local policies. Decisions on content are largely left with headteachers and assistants, and whatever general trends emerge in the curriculum are generated within the educational subculture.

A profession has a code of ethics. The independent professions lay down for their members a code of ethics which, in Lieberman's terms 'has been clarified and interpreted at ambiguous points by concrete cases'. Such codes are concerned with prescribing appropriate relationships between practitioner and client which will protect the client, and between the practitioners themselves for their mutual protection. The National Union of Teachers has drawn up a code which defines a number of forms of unprofessional behaviour, mostly concerned with protecting the teacher and the Union. But in the absence of a professionally-controlled licensing body in education such a code can act as a guide to conduct but cannot be enforced, although, of course, the Union can terminate a teacher's membership, but not his right to teach.

A profession generates in-service growth. Because a profession is founded upon a body of knowledge and skill which is constantly changing, an important criterion is that it should foster the in-service growth of its practitioners. Comparisons between professions as to the degree of in-service development which its members

84

accomplish are difficult to make, but certainly each profession has its research element, its *avant garde*, and its means of disseminating new knowledge. The in-service training of teachers has been rapidly growing in recent years, and many courses, conferences, workshops and training sessions have been organized by the Department of Education and Science, local authorities, universities, colleges and other bodies, and as opportunities for full-time and part-time participation increases for teachers, it may well become the norm rather than the exception to participate in some in-service programme. In addition, there has been a rapid growth in educational research carried out by the National Foundation for Educational Research, universities, and other bodies, a recent emergence of curriculum development centres for teachers, and an increase in the activities of professional associations concerned with various aspects of the curriculum. All this activity has led to a growing awareness of the significance of the relevance to teaching of quite basic research in psychology, sociology, philosophy and curriculum.

It would appear from the above discussion that education fulfils in part most of the main criteria of a profession, but falls short of the standing achieved by such professions as medicine and law. But it should also be noted that the independent professions themselves are undergoing change. More of their practitioners are working in organizations and are thus becoming subject to more bureaucratic control, the work of these professions is coming more under public scrutiny and control, and their professional organizations are beginning to take on some of the militancy of trade protection associations. Thus whilst there are still a number of directions in which teaching can seek to improve its status, it may well be that the more autonomous professions are themselves moving closer towards the present position of teaching.

Barriers to professional status

Having noted that teaching meets the more widely accepted criteria of a profession partly but not fully, we can turn to the miscellaneous factors which could be acting as barriers to its advancement.

The social class background of entrants to the profession. The standing of a profession is to some extent affected by the social class background of its recruits; the higher the social strata from which recruits generally come, the higher the status of the profession. And, of course, the higher the status of a profession the more it will attract recruits from the higher social strata. Entry into teaching has been one means of upward social mobility for the intelligent working class individual, and undoubtedly the preponderance of working class recruits to the former elementary schools—the picture is rather different for public and grammar schools—has acted as a brake upon the improvement of the status of the profession. But a study carried out in 1955 (Floud and Scott, 1961) showed that since the last war the proportion of teachers with working class origins was in decline in the primary and non-selective schools, but increasing in the selective schools. But a new factor in the situation is the growing recruitment to teaching, via colleges for mature students, of people who have previously worked in other occupations. It would appear that these recruits are more pronouncedly working class in origin than students recruited at eighteen (Altman, 1967).

The attitude towards the recruitment of intelligent working-class boys to some of the independent professions can perhaps be gauged from the following extract from the evidence of the Royal College of Surgeons to the Royal Commission on Doctors' and Dentists' Remuneration, 1958:

Medicine would lose immeasurably if the proportion of (middle-class) students in the future were to be reduced in favour of precocious children who qualified for subsidies from local authorities and the State, purely on the basis of examination results. (Quoted by Cotgrove, 1962).

Such attitudes might, in the past, have worked in favour of a higher level of ability, if not of higher prestige, in the teaching profession, but as we move from an ascriptive to an achievement oriented society we might expect such social barriers to be lowered. Yet with what consequences for the teaching profession it is hard to foretell.

Balance between the sexes in teaching. Teaching recruits a higher preponderance of women than men, and in spite of the drop-out of women in their early years of teaching they constitute 60 per cent of the full-time teaching force. And although there has been a steady improvement in the social status of women in our society since the nineteenth century, the preponderance of women in the teaching profession is likely to detract from its status for men. It is important to emphasize the sex difference here, and also the difference in status between the individual and the profession. Teaching has a relatively high status in the occupations usually followed by women, but a relatively lower status amongst occupations normally followed by men. Thus the social standing of a woman teacher may be higher than the relative social standing of a male teacher. The general status of the profession, compared with other professional occupations which are usually dominated by males, is diminished through the preponderance of women. This may not necessarily be due to any notion of the inferior abilities of women compared with men, although no doubt such ideas will prevail, but because of what Caplow (1954) has termed the 'special conditions' attaching to female employment such as the fact that their careers are often intermittent, that they are usually only secondary breadwinners in the family, that they tend to be residentially immobile, and that cultural norms discriminate against appointment of women to superior positions over men.

Commitment to profession. Membership of the major professions implies a life commitment to the task, and one barrier to the improvement of the prestige of teaching is that such a life commitment to the task of teaching is not as apparent as in other professions. A number of factors contribute to this. One of these, following from the previous point, is the intermittent career pattern of married women. Another is the general notion of teaching as a 'second choice' profession with many graduates only commiting themselves to it at a late stage, and with an increasing intake of people who have followed other occupations. A third factor, and one which will be discussed in more detail in a separate context at a later point, is that upward mobility within the profession will often take the individual practitioner out of the classroom and perhaps the school. An American study by Mason (1961) showed that half of a sample of teachers at the beginning of their careers did not expect to stay in teaching for more than five years.

Salary. The salary level enjoyed by a profession may be partly a measure of the esteem in which the profession is held in society, partly a reflection of the relative scarcity of the skills required in the practice of the profession, and partly a reflection of the power which the organized profession can exercise in its own interests. Although the economic status of the teacher —especially the woman teacher—has been steadily improving, teachers do not in general receive salaries comparable to those received within the major professions. It has already been noted that there is some ambivalence in society concerning the esteem of teachers and the nature of the skills and knowledge required for the task of teaching. And although the teachers' unions have fought a long and relatively successful campaign for improvements in the pay and conditions of teachers (Tropp, 1957), they have not apparently been able to wield the same degree of power as the organized medical profession. One factor which perhaps prevents a more rapid increase in the salaries of teachers is that whereas the social functions of the doctor and the lawyer are immediate and clear since they are constantly dealing with what are crucial issues for their individual clients, the functions and responsibilities of the teacher are more diffuse, effective only over a longer time scale, and part of a 'normal' process which is experienced by everyone (Wilson, 1962).

The nature of the final award. The final academic award obtained by the majority of members of a profession can be regarded as a general indication of its intellectual standards. At the present time it is only a minority of the teaching profession which possesses a university degree, and this factor must depress the status of the profession. In recognition of this fact the teachers' unions have long advocated a graduate profession and a further step has been taken towards this with the introduction of the B.Ed. degree—although at the present time this is taken only by a small minority of college of education students. But in view of the fact that the certificate in education which is awarded by the colleges is still widely considered simply as a recognition of classroom competence, the B.Ed. degree, through its designation as a degree in 'education' rather than in one of the basic academic disciplines, may only slowly come to be recognized for what it represents—in spite of its similarities with the medical degree.

It would appear from the above discussion that there remain some quite considerable barriers to the improvement of the status of teaching as a profession. This presents the teachers' unions with a dilemma. They can choose to pursue what Lieberman has termed the 'vocational objectives' of a profession, i.e. the improvement in the pay, conditions, and status of their members, or its 'service objectives', i.e. its duties and responsibilities towards society. It is clear that the two are not independent. As Lieberman points out, a profession which has attained a high status in society will be better fitted to perform its service functions, and the higher an individual's income the more likely he is to be devoted to his work for its own sake—one of the characteristics of a professional person. But the problem facing the teachers' unions is whether to emphasize service objectives and trust that society will reward the profession for its responsible approach to its task, or whether to take militant action in support of a truly professional rate of pay which would induce a greater professional orientation to the social functions of education in the long run, but in the short run would deviate from its service objectives. The emphasis in the past has perhaps been upon vocational objectives rather than on service objectives, but there has been some ambivalence about this and one commentator has written of the N.U.T. that at one and the same time 'it behaves with the responsibility of a professional group dedicated to the standards of its own professional work, and at another acts as a straightforward trade union'. (Raison, 1966). The insecurity induced by this dilemma can perhaps be seen in the objections of the unions to the setting up of the Schools Council which was seen by them as a potential threat to the professional autonomy of the teacher, but was seen by many outside the profession as potentially leading to an improvement in the curriculum with the objections of the teachers' unions seen as a defence of vested interests. With increasing opportunities for teachers to participate in educational decision-making, it may well happen that the unions will be in a stronger position to improve the status of the profession by attending more to its service objectives.

The professional culture in education

The members of a profession interact during their training, in their places of employment, within their professional associations, and also informally. And through these interactions a profession generates a distinctive culture embracing its fundamental *values*, the *norms* which govern the behaviour of members, and its *symbols* —including its history, folklore, special vocabulary, insignia, and stereotypes (Greenwood, 1962). This culture is the source of professional solidarity, self-esteem, and self-consciousness. Although a profession may be differentiated in terms of the tasks which its members perform, the professional culture is a source of unity. The 'culture' of the teaching profession has not been widely studied and there are many aspects of it about which more knowledge would be welcome. In particular it would be useful to learn more about the degree of integration and shared assumptions between the different parts; infant, primary and secondary. Lieberman has suggested that primary teaching and secondary teaching could almost be regarded as distinct professions. Likewise it is important to determine the extent of the 'consciousness of kind' between schoolteachers, college of education lecturers, university lecturers, educational administrators, organizers and inspectors. Can we, in fact, speak meaningfully about an 'education profession' which is more extensive than the teaching profession? Or is the culture of some of these potential components of an education profession so divergent from that of others that it would make little sense to talk about shared values? These are important questions and one can only speculate about the answers. It might well be, for example, that there is a suspicion, and perhaps even a hostility, between teachers in different kinds of school, and between those who teach and those who lecture, administer or undertake educational research, which undermines the entire educational enterprise. This could perhaps only be overcome through a common training for all engaged in education, a career structure which encourages a greater commitment to teaching, and a rationalization of criteria for promotion within all branches of education.

The teaching career

The concept of 'career' implies both the notion of a commitment to a form of life-work or 'calling' and the process whereby an individual progresses upwards through a hierarchy of professional roles. These two different connotations serve to reveal an important source of conflict in the teaching role, for to some degree they are incompatible. Upward mobility in the teaching profession often requires a teacher to leave the classroom for an administrative role in the school or within the local authority, for college or university lecturing, for the Inspectorate, for a research post, or for any one of a number of other possibilities. Achievement in our society is usually assessed by one's upward occupational mobility and increase in salary rather than by the less visible skilled performance in one's work. The general aspiration to leave classroom teaching—especially amongst men teachers—is hardly surprising since it is in conformity with one of the central achievement values of our society, and one which they have probably sought to instil into their pupils. But this career pattern generates three problems. The first is that it tends to create the division within the education profession between those who teach and those who do not which was discussed above. The second is that it creates the possibility that the teacher's aspiration to move out of the classroom as a step in his career might serve to reduce his commitment to teaching as he approaches the point of moving out. There is some safeguard here in that promotion is notionally dependent upon demonstrated teaching ability, but as the criteria for promotion are rather unclear a decline in commitment might not necessarily be a barrier to promotion. A third problem is that when the skilful and committed teacher leaves the classroom he may do so only reluctantly in conformity with the 'accepted' career pattern. Yet he may experience frustrations and perhaps even some guilt as he performs his new role, away, as it were, from the heat of the battle. These problems can never, of course, be fully overcome, but something might be achieved by creating a career structure for classroom teachers which, at its top end, runs parallel to the career structure outside the classroom rather than, as now, is preliminary to it.

Conclusion

The term 'profession' is less analytic than symbolic and represents the rights and privileges which an occupation desires for itself and also the social service which it offers. We can, however, get some indication of the social standing of an occupation by examining the extent to which it meets certain criteria of a profession derived from those occupations which are clearly recognized as such. Teaching meets many of the accepted criteria in part but not in full, and there still remain some quite significant barriers to the achievement of full professional status. Nevertheless the organized teaching profession might well improve its social standing by placing a greater emphasis on its 'service objectives' and thereby acquiring a stronger voice in the making of educational policy. This voice would probably be strengthened if the *education* profession, rather than the *teaching* profession, was able to develop a set of more widely shared values. But such a situation could probably only arise if there was a reconsideration of patterns of training, career structure, salary structure, and criteria for promotion.

Postscript

This book has been concerned with the typical role of the teacher in Great Britain at the present time. But there are many changes occurring within education and within society as a whole which are beginning to lead to a re-definition of the role, and one would expect that the picture presented here would become out of date within the next few years.

Schools are beginning to change radically in their internal structure. In particular, many schools are experimenting with teaching units varying greatly in size and introducing team teaching. Some of the newer schools are being designed with such flexibility in mind. Thus the notion of the single teacher working with, or perhaps 'performing to', a class of approximately thirty-five may soon be completely outmoded. Such a change would demand a greater co-operation between teachers and a reconsideration of the idea of the teacher as king of his own classroom domain, and to some extent his autonomy will be sacrificed in the interests of integration with other teachers. It has been suggested that in order to make a real impact upon schools in depressed areas, teachers may need to be trained not as individuals but as cadres to go into schools an already integrated and functioning team.

New techniques of instruction such as closed circuit television, teaching machines and language laboratories, and new approaches to an 'open-ended' curriculum, are inevitably going to change the relationship between the teacher and the class unit. As learning becomes more individualized, the teacher will move from the centre of the classroom 'stage' to the periphery as the emphasis swings from teaching to learning. The teacher's skills will be turned more towards programming the learning process and away from 'declamation'.

A new set of variations on the teaching role is emerging including counsellors, teacher-social workers, and curriculum development leaders. Again it is clear that the effectiveness of such roles is dependent upon their integration with other teaching roles. And the orthodox teacher's role itself is expanding to embrace a more direct relationship with the home.

Bernstein (1967) has written of these changes:

> There has been a shift from a teaching role which is, so to speak, 'given' (in the sense that one steps into assigned duties), to a role which has to be *achieved* in relation with other teachers. It is a role which is no longer made but *has to be made*.

Such changes will generate many uncertainties and anxieties for the teacher, and these can only be modified by building up the teacher's professional self-confidence and enhancing his social status.

Further reading

Reference has been made in the text to the main books and articles dealing with the role of the teacher, and the Bibliography can be used as a guide to further study. However, the following works can be specially recommended as core reading on this topic.

A good review of the field is contained in L. J. Westwood, 'The role of the teacher', *Educational Research*, Vols. 9 and 10, 1967, 1968. On the role of the teacher in contemporary society see particularly B. Wilson 'The role of the teacher', *British Journal of Sociology*, Vol. 13, 1962; J. Floud 'The teacher in the affluent society', *British Journal of Sociology*, Vol. 13, 1962; and J. Kob, 'The teacher in industrial society', *Yearbook of Education*, 1963. Although written in 1932 with specific reference to American schools, Willard Waller, *The Sociology of Teaching* remains a minor classic containing many relevant insights into the role of the contemporary teacher. The status of the teacher is discussed in the following: A. Tropp, *The School Teachers*; G. Baron and A. Tropp, 'Teachers in England and America' in A. G. Halsey, et al, *Education, Economy and Society*; and W. Taylor *The Secondary Modern School*. Two empirical studies carried out in Britain are the following: F. Musgrove and P. Taylor, 'Teachers' and parents' conceptions of the teacher's role', *British Journal of Educational Psychology*, Vol. 35, 1965 and D. S. Finlayson and L. Cohen, 'The teacher's role: a comparative study of the conceptions of college of education students and headteachers' *British Journal of Educational Psychology*, Vol. 37, 1967. The most comprehensive treatment of the professional aspects of the role of the teacher is M. Lieberman, *Education as a Profession*. Advanced students and those who are particularly interested in the methodology of role studies should consult: B. Biddle and E. J. Thomas, eds. *Role Theory: Concepts and Research*, Wiley, 1966; N. Gross, W. S. Mason and A. W. McEachern, *Explorations in Role Analysis*; N. Gross and R. Herriott, *Staff Leadership in the Public School*; and B. Biddle, et al., *Studies in the Role of the Public School Teacher*.

Bibliography

ALTMAN, E. (1967) 'The Mature Student Teacher,' *New Society*, 10 (274), 28 December, 1967.

BANKS, OLIVE (1965) *Parity and Prestige in English Secondary Education*, London: Routledge and Kegan Paul.

BANTOCK, G. H. (1963) *Education in an Industrial Society*, London: Faber.

BANTOCK, G. H. (1965) *Education and Values*, London: Faber.

BARON, G. (1954) 'The Teachers' Registration Movement', *British Journal of Educational Studies*, 2(2), 1954.

BARON, G. (1956) 'Some Aspects of the Headmaster Tradition', *Researches and Studies*, June, 1956.

BARON, G. (1964) 'A British View of Brimstone', *Teachers' College Record*, 66, 1964.

BARON, G. and TROPP, A. (1961) 'Teachers in England and America', in HALSEY, A. H., FLOUD, J., and ANDERSON, C. A. eds. *Education, Economy and Society*, New York: Free Press.

BECKER, H. (1962) 'The Teacher in the Authority System of the Public School' in ETZIONI, A. ed. *Complex Organisations: a Sociological Reader*, New York: Holt, Rinehart, Winston.

BERNSTEIN, B. (1961) 'Social Class and Linguistic Development', in HALSEY, A. H., FLOUD, J., and ANDERSON, C. A. *Education, Economy and Society*, New York: Free Press.

BERNSTEIN, B. (1967) 'Open Schools, Open Society?' *New Society* 10 (259) 14 September, 1967.

BIDDLE, B. et al, (1961) *Studies in the Role of the Public School Teacher*, 5 Vols. Columbia: University of Missouri Press.

BIDWELL, C. (1965) 'The School as a Formal Organization' in MARCH, J. G. *Handbook of Organizations*, New York: Rand McNally.

BLYTH, W. A. L. (1965) *English Primary Education*, 2 Vols. London: Routledge and Kegan Paul.

CANNON, C. (1964) 'Some Variations on the Teacher's Role', *Education for Teaching*, May, 1964.

CAPLOW, T. (1954) *The Sociology of Work*, Minneapolis: University of Minnesota Press.

CLARK, B. (1961) 'The Cooling-out Function in Higher Education', in HALSEY, A. H., FLOUD, J. and ANDERSON, C. A. *Education, Economy and Society*, New York: Free Press.

COHEN, A. K. (1955) *Delinquent Boys*, London: Routledge and Kegan Paul.

COLEMAN, J. S. (1961) *Adolescent Society*, New York: Free Press.

CORWIN, R. G. (1965) *A Sociology of Education*, New York: Appleton, Century, Crofts.

COTGROVE, S. (1958) *Technical Education and Social Change*, London: Allen and Unwin.

CRAFT, M., COHEN, L. and RAYNOR, J. eds. (1967) *Linking Home and School*, London: Longmans.

CUNNINGHAM, R. et al (1951) *Understanding Group Behaviour of Boys and Girls*, New York: Teachers' College, Columbia University.

DORE, R. (1965) *Education in Tokugawa Japan*, London: Routledge and Kegan Paul.

DOUGLAS, J. W. B. (1964) *The Home and the School*, London: MacGibbon and Kee.

DURKHEIM, E. (1961) *Moral Education*, New York: Free Press.

ELVIN, L. (1963) 'Comments on the Address given by Mr. D. H. Morrell' *Educational Research* 5 (2) 1963.

EVANS, K. (1962) *Sociometry and Education*, London: Routledge and Kegan Paul.

FINLAYSON, D. S. and COHEN, L. (1967) 'The Teacher's Role: a Comparative Study of the Conceptions of College of Education Students and Head Teachers, *British Journal of Educational Psychology* 37 (1) February, 1967.

FLANDERS, N. (1960) 'Diagnosing and Utilizing Social Structures in Classroom Learning' in *The Dynamics of Instructional Groups*, 59th Yearbook of the National Society for the Study of Education, Chicago: University of Chicago Press.

FLOUD, J. (1962) 'Teaching in the Affluent Society' *British Journal of Sociology*, 13, 1962.

FLOUD, J. and HALSEY, A. H. (1961) 'Intelligence Tests, Social Class and Selection for Secondary Schools in HALSEY, A. H., FLOUD, J. and ANDERSON, C. A. *Education, Economy and Society*, New York: Free Press.

FLOUD, J., HALSEY, A. H. and MARTIN, F. M. (1956) *Social Class and Educational Opportunity*, London: Heinemann.

FLOUD, J. and SCOTT, W. (1961) 'Recruitment to Teaching in England and Wales in HALSEY, A. H., FLOUD, J. and ANDERSON, C. A. *Education, Economy and Society*, New York: Free Press.

FRASER, E. D. (1959) *Home Environment and the School*, London: University of London Press.

GARDNER, J. W. (1961) *Excellence: Can We Be Equal and Excellent Too?* New York: Harper.

GEER, B. (1966) 'Occupational Commitment and the Teaching Profession, *School Review*, 74, 1966.

GETZELS, J. and GUBA, E. G. (1957) 'Social Behaviour and the Administrative Process', *School Review*, 34, 1957.

GETZELS, J. and THELEN, H. A. (1960) 'The Classroom Group as a Unique Social System' in *The Dynamics of Instructional Groups*, 59th Yearbook of the National Society for the Study of Education, Chicago: University of Chicago Press.

GORDON, C. W. (1964) 'The Sociology of Education' in KNELLER, G. F. *Foundations of Education*, New York: Wiley.

GOULDNER, A. W. (1957-8) 'Cosmopolitans and Locals: Towards an Analysis of Latent Social Roles', *Administrative Science Quarterly*, 2, 1957-8.

GREENWOOD, E. (1962) 'Attributes of a Profession' in NOSOW S. and FORM, W. H. *Man, Work and Society*, New York: Basic Books.

HALPIN, A. W. (1966) *Theory and Research in Administration*, New York: Macmillan.

HALSEY, A. H. (1963) 'The Sociology of Moral Education', in NIBLETT, W. R. ed. *Moral Education in a Changing Society*, London: Faber.

HANS, N. (1951) *New Trends in Education in the Eighteenth Century*, London: Routledge and Kegan Paul.

HARGREAVES, D. H. (1967) *Social Relations in a Secondary School*, London: Routledge and Kegan Paul.

HART, C. W. M. (1963) 'Contrasts Between Pre-pubertal and Post-pubertal Education', in SPINDLER, G. ed. *Education and Culture*, New York: Holt, Rinehart, Winston.

HAVIGHURST, R. J. and NEUGARTEN, B. (1962) *Society and Education*, 2nd Ed. New York: Allyn and Bacon.

HEMPHILL, J. K. and COONS, A. E. (1957) 'Leader Behaviour Description Questionnaire', in STOGDHILL, R. M. and COONS, A. E., *Leader Behaviour: Its Description and Measurement*, Columbus, Ohio: Ohio State University Press.

HENRY, J. (1955) 'Docility, Or Giving Teacher What She Wants', *Journal of Social Issues*, 2, 1955.

H.M.S.O. (1967) *Children and their Primary Schools*, London: H.M.S.O.

HOFSTADTER, R. (1962) *Anti-intellectualism in American Life*, London: Cape.

HUGHES, E. C. (1958) *Men and their Work*, Glencoe: Free Press.

IANNACCONE, I. (1964) 'An Approach to the Informal Organization of the School' in *Behavioural Science and Educational Administration*, 63rd Yearbook of the National Society for the Study of Education, Chicago: University of Chicago Press.

JACKSON, B. and MARSDEN, D. (1962) *Education and the Working Class*, London: Routledge and Kegan Paul.

KERR, M. (1958) *The People of Ship Street*, London: Routledge and Kegan Paul.

KISIEL, C. A. (1966) 'Some Perspectives on the Role of the German Teacher', *School Review*, 74, 1966.

KOB, J. (1961) 'Definition of the Teacher's Role' in HALSEY, A. H., FLOUD, J. and ANDERSON, C. A. *Education, Economy and Society*, New York: Free Press.

KOB, J. (1963) 'The Teacher in Industrial Society', *Yearbook of Education*, London: Evans.

LIEBERMAN, M. (1956) *Education as a Profession*, Englewood Cliffs, New Jersey: Prentice Hall.

LIPSET, S. M. (1963) *The First New Nation*, London: Heinemann.

MARSHALL, T. H. (1950) *Citizenship and Social Class*, London: Cambridge University Press.

MASON, W. S., DRESSEL, R. J. and BAIN, R. K. (1959) 'Sex Role and Career Orientation of Beginning Teachers' *Harvard Educational Review*, 29 (4), 1959.

MEAD, M. (1961) 'The School in American Culture' in HALSEY, A. H., FLOUD, J. and ANDERSON, C. A. *Education, Economy and Society*, New York: Free Press.

MEAD, M. (1963) 'Our Educational Emphases in Primitive Perspective' in SPINDLER, D. G. *Education and Culture*, New York: Holt, Rinehart, Winston .

MERTON, R. K. (1956), 'The Role Set', *British Journal of Sociology*, 7, 1956.

MILLERSON, G. (1964) *The Qualifying Associations*, London: Routledge ánd Kegan Paul.

MORRELL, D. (1963) 'The Functions of the Teacher in Relation to Research and Development Work in the Area of the Curriculum and Examinations', *Educational Research*, 5 (2), 1963.

MUSGROVE, F. and TAYLOR, P. H. (1965) 'Teachers' and Parents' Conception of the Teachers' Role', *British Journal of Educational Psychology*, 35, 1965.

PAGE, C. (1951) 'Bureaucracy in Higher Education', *Journal of General Education*, 5, 1951.

PARSONS, T. (1951) *The Social System*, London: Routledge and Kegan Paul.

PARSONS, T. (1961) 'The School Class as a Social System', in HALSEY, A. H., FLOUD, J. and ANDERSON, C. A. *Education, Economy and Society*, New York: Free Press.

PARSONS, T. (1966) *Societies: Evolutionary and Comparative Perspectives*, Englewood Cliffs, New Jersey: Prentice Hall.

PETERS, R. S. (1966) *Ethics and Education*, London: Allen and Unwin.

PHILLIPS, M. (1964) *Small Social Groups in Modern England*, London: Allen and Unwin.

PRESTHUS, R. (1962) *The Organizational Society*, New York: Knopf.

RAISON, T. (1966) 'In Defence of the Professions', *New Society*, 8 (203), 18 August, 1966.

REDL, F. and WATTENBERG, W. (1951) *Mental Hygiene in Teaching*, New York: Harcourt, Brace.

RIESMAN, D. (1957) 'Teachers as a Counter-Cyclical Influence', *School Review*, 65, 1957.

SCHELSKY, H. (1961) 'Family and School in Modern Society', in HALSEY, A. H., FLOUD, J. and ANDERSON, C. A. *Education, Economy and Society*, New York: Free Press.

SOLES, S. (1964) 'Teacher Role Expectations and the Organization of the School', *Journal of Educational Research*, 57, 1964.

SPINDLER, G. D. (1963) 'The Role of the School Administrator' in SPINDLER, G. D. ed. *Education and Culture*, New York : Holt, Rinehart, Winston.

STONES, E. (1963) 'The Role of the Headteacher in English Education', *Forum*, 6, 1963.

SWIFT, D. F. (1967) 'Family Environment and 11 + Success : Some Basic Predictors', *British Journal of Educational Psychology*, 37, 1967.

TAYLOR, W. (1963) *The Secondary Modern School*, London : Faber.

TAYLOR, W. (1966) The Use of Simulation in the In-Service Training of Educational Administrators in England', *Journal of Educational Administration*, 4, 1966.

TERRIEN, F. W. (1953) 'Who Thinks What About Educators?' *American Journal of Sociology*, 59, 1953.

THELEN, H. A. (1954) *Dynamics of Groups at Work*, Chicago : University of Chicago Press.

TROPP, A. (1957) *The School Teachers*, London : Heinemann.

TURNER, R. H. (1961) 'Modes of Social Ascent Through Education', in HALSEY, A. H., FLOUD, J. and ANDERSON, C. A. *Education, Economy and Society*, New York : Free Press.

WALLER, W. (1932) *The Sociology of Teaching*, New York : Wiley.

WATKINS, M. H. (1963) 'The West African Bush School', in SPINDLER, G. D. *Education and Culture*, New York : Holt, Rinehart, Winston.

WEBB, J. (1962) 'The Sociology of a School', *British Journal of Sociology*, 13, 1962.

WESTWOOD, L. J. (1966) 'Reassessing the Role of the Head', *Education for Teaching*, 1966.

WILCOX, P. (1967) 'The School and the Community', *The Record*, 9 (2), 1967.

WILKINSON, A. (1966) 'English in the Training of Teachers', *Universities Quarterly*, 20 (3), 1966.

WILKINSON, R. (1964) *The Prefects*, London : Heinemann.

WILLIAMS, R. (1961) *The Long Revolution*, London : Chatto and Windus.

WILSON, B. (1962) 'The Teacher's Role : a Sociological Analysis', *British Journal of Sociology*, 13, 1962.

WILSON, B. (1966) 'An Approach to Delinquency', *New Society*, 7 (176), 3 February, 1966.

YOUNG, M. (1958) *The Rise of the Meritocracy*, London : Macgibbon and Kee.

Students Library of Education

General Editor   Lionel Elvin

The Foundations of Twentieth-Century Education. E. Eaglesham. 128 pp.

The French Influence on English Education. W. H. G. Armytage. 128 pp.

*The German Influence on English Education. W. H. G. Armytage. 142 pp.

Mediaeval Education and the Reformation. J. Lawson. 128 pp.

Recent Education from Local Sources. Malcolm Seaborne. 128 pp.

*The Russian Influence on English Education. W. H. G. Armytage. 138 pp.

Secondary School Reorganization in England and Wales. Alun Griffiths. 128 pp.

Social Change and the Schools: 1918–1944. Gerald Bernbaum. 128 pp.

The Social Origins of English Education. Joan Simon. 132 pp.

PHILOSOPHY

Education and the Concept of Mental Health. John Wilson. 99 pp.

Indoctrination and Education. I. A. Snook. 128 pp.

Interest and Discipline in Education. P. S. Wilson. 142 pp.

The Logic of Education. P. H. Hirst and R. S. Peters. 196 pp.

Philosophy and the Teacher. Edited by D. I. Lloyd. 180 pp.

The Philosophy of Primary Education. R. F. Dearden. 208 pp.

Plato and Education. Robin Barrow. 96 pp.

Problems in Primary Education. R. F. Dearden. 160 pp.

PSYCHOLOGY

Creativity and Education. Hugh Lytton. 144 pp.

Group Study for Teachers. Elizabeth Richardson. 144 pp.

Human Learning: A Developmental Analysis. H. S. N. McFarland. 136 pp.

An Introduction to Educational Measurement. D. Pidgeon and A. Yates. 122 pp.

Modern Educational Psychology: An Historical Introduction. E. G. S. Evans. 118 pp.

An Outline of Piaget's Developmental Psychology. Ruth M. Beard. 144 pp.

Personality, Learning and Teaching. George D. Handley. 126 pp.

*Teacher Expectations and Pupil Learning. Roy Nash. 128 pp.

Teacher and Pupil: Some Socio-Psychological Aspects. Philip Gammage. 128 pp.

Troublesome Children in Class. Irene E. Caspari. 160 pp.

SOCIOLOGY

Basic Readings in the Sociology of Education. D. F. Swift. 368 pp.
Class, Culture and the Curriculum. Denis Lawton. 140 pp.
Culture, Industrialisation and Education. G. H. Bantock. 108 pp.
*Education at Home and Abroad. Joseph Lauwerys and Graham Tayar. 144 pp.
Education, Work and Leisure. Harold Entwistle. 118 pp.
The Organization of Schooling: A Study of Educational Grouping Practices. Alfred Yates. 116 pp.
*Political Education in a Democracy. Harold Entwistle. 144 pp.
The Role of the Pupil. Barbara Calvert. 160 pp.
The Role of the Teacher. Eric Hoyle. 112 pp.
The Social Context of the School. S. John Eggleston. 128 pp.
The Sociology of Educational Ideas. Julia Evetts. 176 pp.

CURRICULUM STUDIES

*Towards a Compulsory Curriculum. J. P. White. 122 pp.

INTERDISCIPLINARY STUDIES

*Educational Theory: An Introduction. T. W. Moore. 116 pp.
Perspectives on Plowden. R. S. Peters. 116 pp.
*The Role of the Head. Edited by R. S. Peters. 136 pp.

* Library edition only